When I Get Old I Plan To Be A Bitch

Aging in Sneakers and Running from Stereotypes

by Cathy Goodwin

When I Get Old I
Plan To Be A Bitch

3Aging in Sneakers and

Running from Stereotype

Copyright © 2022 By Cathy Goodwin

ISBN 978-1-7324400-1-2

Library of Congress Control Number: 2022910853

When I Get Old I Plan To Be A Bitch

Aging in Sneakers and Running from Stereotypes

Contents

Introduction

"Growing old isn't on anyone's list of 10 things to do before I die."

"I've learned now, if somebody calls me a bitch, to say thank you. Because the reason they're calling you a bitch is usually something to be proud of." Gloria Steinem

"I would honestly rather read a romance novel than read one more book about aging." — Goodreads comment on *Elderhood* by Louise Aronson

It happens gradually, like summer to fall during an Indian summer in Philadelphia, one leaf at a time.

While everything is still green, I know exactly who I am.

I am happily carrying on, business as usual, working on the Internet. I'm the one everybody calls when their website is screwed up and their tech has disappeared. I'm the one working out in the gym religiously on Sunday mornings. I take the dog for long walks. I avoid doctors. I dress the way I've done most of my adult life: jeans or leggings in winter, shorts in summer. In fifteen years, my feet haven't seen anything stiffer than a sneaker (except for three hours at a friend's wedding, when I crammed my innocent toes into a "dressy flat").

But then fall comes, one leaf at a time. Every so often I feel like someone who walked out of the house in a Halloween costume and forgot I was wearing it.

Or I feel like the characters in the old Showtime series, Dead Like Me: they're dead and they feel the same, but other people see an unrecognizable, uglier version of their former selves.

Or the Bruce Willis character in Sixth Sense: he feels alive even though he's dead. And nobody sees him.

Or I'm talking to someone at a party. She's a nurse and I'm sharing my experience of the last time I'd been in a medical setting. Suddenly I notice she's giving me The Look...that "how cute you are" smirk that people save for older people and puppies. She's got that patronizing little smile. She's nodding. She's giving me that glazed "I'm humoring her" look.

Or somebody notices I take the stairs slowly -- like I've done all my life, following a nearly outgrown childhood phobia. I can read their minds: "Frail old lady."

"It's all about expectations"

In her book, *Out of Time*, Lynn Segal quotes from a novel by Julian Barnes, *Staring At the Sun*. His female heroine muses:

"You grow old first not in your own eyes, but in other people's eyes; then, slowly, you agreed with their opinion of you. It wasn't that you couldn't walk as far as you used to, it was that other

people didn't expect you to; and if they didn't, then it needed vain obstinacy to persist."

There's the time a young woman in the weight room of my gym calls out, "Looking good! Keep it up."

A compliment, except that I'm working with the lat pulldown -- one of the easiest pieces of equipment in the gym, the one you're taught first when you take a weight training class. I don't even pile on much weight. She was really saying, "Not bad for an old broad."

Or the day I'm happily hip-swiveling in a Zumba class, when the young woman next to me says condescendingly, "You look like you're having fun." It's the tone someone might use with a child who needs encouragement.

Or the doctor who dismisses my exercise injury with, "What can you expect from your knees at your age?"

And then it dawns on me. I'm old. I just don't know it yet. And I'm in deep denial.

When a younger woman asks, "What's your secret?" I tell her I work out 3 times a week, stay away from doctors, and swear like a sailor. She never asks me again.

One day I attend an alumni book discussion at the University of Pennsylvania, just across town. I mention that I've reviewed the book we're talking about. Afterward, a woman who seems close to my age says, "How nice that you're still writing book reviews."

Do I say, "Honey, I don't just write book reviews. I write books."

Or do I say, "Ruth Bader Ginsburg was a lot older than I am when she died. She was *still* writing legal opinions -- just a tad more complex than a few book reviews."

You never read about these subtly cruel encounters in those chirpy articles proclaiming, "Age is just a number." Or "You're only as old as you feel." Or, as John Leland's book title says, "Happiness is a choice."

"Age was my defining characteristic."

Nell Irvin Painter's book, *Old in Art School*, chronicles her experience of attending art school at Rutgers University. The school was noted, she says, for welcoming students of diverse colors, genders, and backgrounds.

Nell herself had been a distinguished historian and professor. She is Black. Yet once she joined the student body, she writes (p.10), "At Rutgers, I stuck out more on account of age than race or quality of attention or personal apparel."

A young female student blurted out, "How old are you?"

"Sixty-four," replied Nell. The student literally gasped … "not hostile, just stunned." Her first reaction was, "OMG, I gotta tell my mom."

OMG is right. Reading this anecdote, I flashed on a memory from my former gym. A young woman, an exchange student from Mexico, said sincerely, "I want to take a picture with you to send my mom." Fortunately, we dispersed to our separate classes and the photo opportunity never happened.

"Sixty-four," Nell continues, "had turned me into a phantasm, a creature from another planet...The crucial fact of my age emerged, not as an incidental, but as my defining characteristic, of how others saw me as a demand to see myself through their eyes."

Being old, Nell says, "summed her up," overshadowing "all the things I had done to become a historian -- a goddamn distinguished historian." That's how, she concludes, she's seen in the eyes of others.

Try this on other demographic groups.

I asked a gay friend, "How would you like to be defined solely by being gay? Instead of Bob the accountant, you're "Bob the gay accountant."

He shuddered. "I'd hate it."

Try "Mary the Asian-American yoga teacher."

Or "Susan the African-American pediatrician, who's really very good, you know."

Offensive? Sure. And so is, "Nell the older art student."

Getting older is supposed to mean being happier - a LOT happier - while making do with a LOT less.

Many authors insist elders have a unique claim on joy. I'm reminded of the pre-Civil War defenses of slaves who were happily singing in their cabins. "See how happy they are?"

Mary Pipher, who's usually displayed great sensitivity on this topic, nevertheless writes in a *New York Times* article:

"We don't expect perfection or even relief from suffering. A good book, a piece of homemade pie, or a call from a friend can make us happy.

Even worse, Pipher quotes her friend: "When I was young, I needed sexual ecstasy or a hike to the top of a mountain to experience bliss. Now I can feel it when I look at a caterpillar on my garden path."

Seriously... a caterpillar?

When I reach that point, you can pour my cold, dead ashes into my urn.

We never used to talk about this.

Aging wasn't a part of my consciousness. I never knew my grandparents; they died before I started kindergarten. With no role models, I couldn't imagine myself growing old. I figured I'd make it to, say, age fifty.

The media didn't offer help either. When I was in my impressionable twenties, *The New York Times* certainly didn't devote whole sections to aging.

Today people over 65 make up a significant part of the population, worldwide. Courses with "Aging" in the title have been offered for popular consumption as well as for health professionals and sociologists. People of a certain age are invited to address medical students, so future doctors can see a real live elderly person walking around.

The downside is, many of us live longer and take longer to die. The days are gone when you could keel over on a street corner on Monday and be firmly underground a week later. Now you can spend a week and a million dollars on life support, emerging as a dependent, helpless shadow of your former self. Our health care system and political infrastructure haven't kept up.

As a result, many millennials have watched their parents struggle to take care of their own aging parents. They're smart to be scared.

Even if you're active and energetic, you face daily insults as you navigate the world. You're encouraged to accept second-class status.

You're supposed to rejoice when you're named Miss Congeniality, knowing the Queen's crown will never be within your reach.

So "growing old" isn't on most people's list of "10 things to do before I die." Many of us want to move directly to "die."

I've learned not to be too quick to share my age. Admittedly I'm horrified when I look at the number, even when I'm alone. But once I tell people I'm sixty, or sixty-four, or seventy, or seventy-four … that's all they remember. The rest of my identity just floats away.

So now when someone says, "Do you mind if I ask how old you are?" I say yes, I absolutely do mind. And I explain exactly why. After reading this book, you may be inspired to do the same.

This book should come with a warning.

This book is not a how-to or self-help book for people growing older. It's about how and why we need to attack the stereotypes associated with aging…which some people experience as young as age 35. It's based on three premises that you won't find in those chirpy books promising, "Age is just a number."

Premise #1: Age is a particularly useless way to predict the behavior of individual adult human beings.

You might say that a certain percentage of people over fifty use prescription drugs, count the days to retirement, or sink gratefully into the sofa after a one-mile walk.

But you can't look at the over-50 woman standing in front of you and make a prediction. In fact, it's dangerous to try.

Geriatricians – the MD's who specialize in care of the "elderly" – have a saying: If you've seen one 80-year-old, you've seen one 80-year-old.

You don't need research to tell you this. In almost every gym, you'll see a group of "older" people walking slowly around a circle in a special class. In the same gym, you'll see people the same age who are training to run marathons.

That sweet little white-haired lady working the leg lift machine? She might have played two sets of tennis this morning. Don't mess with her.

Later I'll talk about the 82-year-old powerlifter Willie Murphy. She beat up a burglar who bought into the belief that "old" means "weak and helpless."

Premise #2: Beliefs about aging can be more powerful and more toxic than physiological realities.

We're taught to believe that old age inevitably means our bodies wear down and our intellects go soft. It's those beliefs - not the actual aging - that accounts for a lot of those changes.

In their book, *Peak: Secrets from the New Science of Expertise*, Anders Ericsson and Robert Pool write that people can "train effectively well into their eighties. Much of the age-related deterioration in various skills happens because people decrease or stop their training; older people who continue to train regularly see their performance decrease much less." (pages 277-278 in the ebook)

Throughout this book, I'll be referring to Ellen Langer's famous experiment. It's described in a *New York Times* article, perfectly titled, "What if Age Is Nothing But a Mindset?" She invited eight men in their seventies to spend two weeks at a monastery where she had created a time warp.

The environment was set with music and magazines from 1959. The men were encouraged to re-experience themselves from twenty-two years ago. "Nothing — no mirrors, no modern-day clothing, no photos except portraits of their much younger selves — spoiled the illusion that they had shaken off 22 years," the article explains.

Just five days later, the men performed better on several physiological measures. Their eyesight was better. Independent observers said they looked better.

Several years later, BBC replicated the study with six former celebrities, both men and women. They obtained similar results. At the outset, one female participant walked shakily, with the help of two canes. Two weeks later, with no medical intervention, she left on her own power with just one cane.

Obviously, some people experience serious mental, financial and physical issues that go beyond these interventions. That's way beyond the scope of this book.

But a very high percentage of people in their 60s, 70s, 80s, and even 90s are held back more by an attitude of, "What can you expect." All too many of them will hear this sentiment from the very people they're supposed to trust, especially their doctors. Eventually it'll become the little voice in the back of their minds...their Inner Old Person.

Premise #3: Stereotypes are not harmless.

Every time you reinforce a stereotype, you're denying someone a job, a friendship, and even an opportunity to live longer.

Stereotypes lead to ridiculous and contradictory attitudes, such as, "Older people have wisdom," yet "Older people aren't smart enough to contribute to the workplace," and even, "Older people shouldn't be trusted to make their own decisions about living and dying."

Stereotypes lead to ineffective and ultimately harmful medical "care." They make an old person's life a living hell...with the best of intentions, of course.

Stereotypes keep older people from living full lives, from working as long as they want to, and from claiming their worth and dignity right to the very end. Stereotypes literally make people sick, as we'll see in the chapters on medical services.

As Nell Irvin Painter wrote in *Old in Art School*:

"There is so much more to me than age...With my energy and excellent health, I routinely refute expectations of the older woman, just as over the years I have grown accustomed to soaring above what was expected of me -- me as a black person, me as a woman, me as a person of my generation. Why wouldn't I be able to go to art school at sixty-four?"

If you find yourself responding to at least one stereotype with, "Oh no - that can't be right," this book will be a success. With practice, you can even add, "Do I look like I give a fuck?"

When you find yourself empowered to fight back against those who characterize you as an uppity old bitch (and they will), you will be on your way to changing your own world and eventually help a lot of others along the way.

Chapter 1:
"I'm not old. I'm a short-timer in life."

"The same behavior may have very different meanings in younger and older people. Much of an older person's behavior may be currently misunderstood as stemming from deficiency rather than choice." - Ellen Langer and Mihnea Moldoveanu.

What if everyone engaged in a lifelong experiment – a version of Ellen Langer's famous "clockwork" study? Stop defining yourself by age. Stop using words like "old" or "as you get older" to explain anything.

"I'm having a senior moment" becomes, "I forgot that person's name," or even, "That's a Freudian slip."

"She's old so she can't understand technology" becomes, "She doesn't see the need to learn technology."

"My back feels sore – I must be getting old" becomes, "My back feels sore – I need a referral to a good physical therapist." Or even, "I did too many reps on the lat pull machine and forgot to do my stretches."

The truth is, most of what we call "old" can be explained by birth cohort effects and short-timer effects.

Birth Cohort Effects

When I was a little girl, I'd ride the city bus to school. On the way home, I'd see older ladies returning from a day of shopping. They seemed to come from another planet. They were unmistakably ladies. They wore smart little dresses with mid-heeled shoes and, heaven help us, nylon stockings. They wore slips and stuffed their tiny little butts into uncomfortable, tight girdles.

"Will this be me someday?" I wondered.

At the time I hadn't heard of the "birth cohort effect." I associated growing older with dressing conservatively and spending a day idly shopping.

It didn't occur to me that this generation of women had always dressed up to go shopping. They viewed shopping as a form of recreation – a special occasion. They wouldn't wear slacks in public, let alone shorts.

By the time I was half their age, they were gone. And sadly, so were most of the department stores they had patronized.

People who enter the world at the same time form a birth cohort. People born around the same group of years form a generation. They have an awful lot in common with each other, for reasons having nothing to do with age.

Once you become aware of cohort effects, you'll begin to see how often they explain away the stereotypes of aging.

In a blog post, "Let's Climb Out Of The Generation Trap," Ashton Applewhite claims that millennial job-hopping is more about age than cohort. Criticizing a whole generation, she says, can promote divisiveness.

That may be true. But when I first entered the job market, "job hopping" most definitely was stigmatized. Today's entry-level workers feel much more comfortable with frequent job changes and frankly, they face a different world. In some fields, five years is considered a long time to spend with one company. Earlier generations didn't have to deal with "temp to perm" as the normal sequence.

When your great-grandmother frowns on swearing, it's not because she's old. It's because she heard, "Nice ladies don't swear," from the first time she innocently brought her brother's language to the family dinner table.

But if you've been swearing since you were eleven years old, you're not likely to stop. Nick Swardson of Comedy Central was credited with saying, "I swear all the time. That's how I'm gonna be when I'm old."

Writing for the Sixty and Me blog, Ann Richardson explains:

"[Our grandmothers] wore sensible shoes and 'appropriate' clothes.

"They mended socks and cooked everything from scratch. They stayed at home or went out with friends to do something sedentary,

like playing bingo or bridge. They would never dream of an exercise class...They seemed old to us, but perhaps more importantly, they felt old to themselves."

Your 70-year-old self will be different from your mother's and grandmother's 70-year-old selves.

Your great-grandmother probably never thought about joining a gym. Women rarely worked out with weights through most of the twentieth century.

But suppose you joined your first gym when you were thirty, and you know how to use all the equipment in the weight room. "Gym membership" will be as much a part of your life as "seeing your dentist." If you're forty now, you can expect to see lots of ninety-year-olds hanging out at the gym with you in fifty years.

Women who turned 70 in 1985 were born in 1915.

They'd lived through a major depression; they were just below kindergarten age as World War I was ending. Men were in their late twenties when World War II broke out, at the upper limit of the draft age.

Women weren't allowed to wear pantsuits to work until they reached their mid-fifties. They grew up with sex discrimination as a fact of life: newspapers openly posted jobs separately for women (and often differentiated by race, too).

16

This generation didn't grow up with swearing, tattoos, and wearing short shorts in public. Women certainly didn't let their bra straps show; they actually wore slips that never dipped below the hemlines of their skirts. If they lived in the United States, they grew up with segregation and would be in their forties when the Civil Rights Act was passed.

Women playing sports? They'd be called tomboys. Interracial marriage and "homosexuality" were illegal for a good part of their lives. Many would grow up without ever meeting a self-professed atheist.

Women who turned 70 in 2015 were born around 1945.

They were born just as World War II had ended. Their parents vividly remembered the Great Depression and may have served in the military during World War II or the Korean War.

They were teenagers when construction began on the Berlin Wall. They went to college when the drinking age was eighteen. Reliable birth control -- "the pill" -- wasn't available until the 1960s,

Most college medical centers wouldn't offer birth control to unmarried students, if they offered it at all. In fact, younger women may not realize that birth control was illegal for married couples in some states until 1965, when the Supreme Court decided the case known as Griswold vs. Connecticut.

Those born in 1945 turned twenty-one during the turbulent sixties. They would have watched news reports of protests related to civil rights and the Vietnam War. Some actively participated. They saw friends and siblings drafted to the war in Vietnam and they may have lost classmates and family members to that war, which was far more controversial than World War II. They may have known men who moved to Canada to escape the draft.

They watched all these events mostly in black and white. Color television wasn't common until the early 1970s.

Women took sex discrimination for granted when they entered the workforce. They heard employers openly talk about "a good job for a woman" while they were in their career-defining twenties. They were 27 when Title IX passed, well past the age of participating in college sports.

Looking ahead, women who will turn 70 in 2045 were born around 1975.

This cohort grew up taking Title IX for granted. They don't remember a world where women couldn't play professional sports, enter military academies or fly airplanes. They don't associate "getting dressed up" with wearing suits. They wear short shorts everywhere and let their bra straps show. They don't associate tattoos or heavy-duty swearing with San Diego sailors; they swear like those sailors and might even show off a few "tats" (unless they're scared of needles like me).

They saw the first gay marriage licenses in 2004, when they were around thirty years old. They'll still experience sex discrimination, but it won't feel normal. And they're quite sophisticated sexually.

Back in 2005, a sociology professor told me, "When I started teaching sociology of sex, students were curious to learn about gay men and lesbians. Now it's no big deal; they all know gay people."

Bottom Line: A 70-year-old will be shaped by her birth cohort much more than her age.

While I'm not crazy about sayings like "70 is the new 50," the truth is that your 70s will be quite different from your mother's 70s. And your grandmother will be even less helpful as a role model.

The Short-Timer Effect

Urban Dictionary elaborates short-timer effect as...

...the behaviors that kick in when you are about to leave something, usually a job. There are two facets, one is that all of the little crap that you've been ignoring and tolerating starts driving you crazy. The other is the idea that you're leaving anyway so you can get away with anything.

When you hit a certain age - somewhere north of 65 - you might wonder how much payback you'll get for your efforts. When you need 5 years to build a business or learn a skill, you wonder, "How much time do I have to enjoy the reward?"

But that's not because you're old.

I once had a conversation with a young woman who survived a particularly deadly form of cancer. She knew she wouldn't recover from a recurrence and she was always aware that death might be close by. She was a short-timer at thirty-two.

My own role model comes from back in the 1960s when an author named John D. Macdonald created a fictional detective hero, Travis McGee.

McGee lived a dangerous life. He took risks. He "found" things for people for astronomical fees. Between clients, he lived on a houseboat in Florida.

McGee knew he might be killed on any assignment. His philosophy was to take his retirement in chunks -- lots of long vacations between jobs, because he might not be around later.

I read the McGee series at a young, impressionable age and adopted his philosophy at once. I took lots of time off in my twenties, thirties, and forties ... which ultimately contributed to a "been-there, done-that" effect at a very early age.

The short-timer effect can become a self-fulfilling prophecy.

Olga Kotelko ran track and field in her nineties. At age 77, she began working with a professional trainer in a gym. She didn't think, "When I'm 85 I probably won't be able to do this." She just moved forward. She was never a short-timer.

I experience the short-timer effect when I think of doing stand-up comedy.

I love performing. When you've got a room roaring with laughter at something you said, it's a high like nothing else.

But there's the downside: long nights in dive clubs, the inevitable night when nobody laughs, waiting for hours to go on for a five-minute spot, and listening to mostly pretty horrible comedy wannabes telling jokes that would be right at home in a college fraternity house.

Joan Rivers was 80 when she died, still performing. But she wasn't starting out. She was enjoying the rewards of her 20s, 30s, and 40s.

Yet if I have to be honest, I'm not really that crazy about investing time to become a better comedian. There's no way I'll drive around to the little places in the suburbs that are more welcoming than the big city venues. I really, really hate waiting five hours to do a five-minute set.

On the other hand, I still work on my business (though I won't put in the hours I did as a college professor - that's part of the "been there, done that" effect). I'm taking online courses in history and science. I study French by reading French murder mysteries and watching French cat videos. I go to the gym and take long walks.

Unlike Olga, I think about the short-timer effect when I make choices…and sometimes I dive in anyway.

Short-timer effects do have a useful role in making medical decisions.

Let's say you're 78 years old. You figure, "In eight to ten years, my circumstances will change drastically." You realize that many – maybe most – people in their mid to late eighties can lose their mind, sight, or mobility.

So now your doctor discovers you have cancer. Should you have surgery, radiation, and chemo?"

As a short-timer, you might think, "It won't make much difference in the long run. I don't want to spend my remaining years dealing with the aftermath of cancer treatment."

Or you might think, "I'd rather die before I end up in a nursing home."

Or you might think, "I'll take my chances. I might be one of the outliers who's strong and healthy in my nineties."

Ezekiel Emanuel's controversial article, "I Want To Die At 75," is a form of the short-timer effect. If your best life ends at 75, why bother?

A lot of "old" behavior is just a mindset.

When I was starting my business, people kept talking about mindset. "Too woo-woo for me," I said. I was looking for techniques.

Now I know that with the right mindset, I'd figure out how to learn whatever I needed.

Carol Dweck's best-selling book, *Mindset: The New Psychology of Success*, introduced many of us to the concept of a growth mindset. If you experience a failure, do you blame yourself? Or do you say, "How can I do better next time?" If you ask the second question, you're demonstrating a growth mindset, suggesting you're likely to experience more success in life.

We've seen the power of mindset in the experiments conducted by Ellen Langer and the BBC. When participants changed their mindset, they also changed their physiology. These experiments also demonstrate the power of "what everyone knows" about growing older.

Age of Champions is a movie about participants in the US Senior Games, including a basketball team for women in their 50s, 60s, and 70s. They laughed when a woman at the airport said, "Basketball? I used to play. Now I'm too old. I'm 42."

Closer to home, a sixty-something woman was taking a tour of the gym where I was a member.

"I can't take those classes at my age," she told the staff member.

I wanted to tell her about the seventy-somethings who were happily jumping around in Zumba.

Chapter 2: "I ain't Miss Congeniality"

"I hate it when they say, "Here's Joan and she's 77 years young. I want to say, here's Vanessa Feltz and she's 350 pounds thin." — Joan Rivers

In a beauty pageant, Miss Congeniality isn't the most beautiful or most talented. She's just *nice*.

She's the one in Kacey Musgraves's song, *Pageant Material*...the one who hugs everyone after she's the fifth runner-up. Not a trace of envy or spite.

Miss Congeniality is the perfect metaphor for the role assigned to older women in the twenty-first century. You miss out on the main event -- earning money at market rates and being taken seriously -- so you get the niceness award.

Instead of being called Miss Congeniality, you get to be called "Grandma."

Like Miss Congeniality, Grandma is nice. She bakes cookies. She spoils the grandchildren. She knits socks. She's kind of fluffy.

Most of all, she's clueless about business and technology. In fact, she's got an "Oh dear, I need help" air about her.

Grandma would never speak out and stand up for herself. She'd certainly never hire a lawyer to protect her rights.

People talk to Grandma like she's five years old. "What do you mean, the doctor's an idiot? You naughty girl! Shut up and take your meds."

Many older women accept this role cheerfully. Even if they don't knit or bake, they believe Grandma serves everyone else at her expense. She's convinced she doesn't really count as a person in her own right.

"Oh no, dear, you take the last piece of cake."

"The doctor's running an hour late? He's probably busy saving the lives of more deserving (i.e., younger) people. I'm grateful he even makes time for me."

Fortunately, those attitudes are going the way of panty girdles, slips, and blue-dyed hair.

"Grandma" has become a generic name for all older women.

If you're really a grandma and you rejoice in that role, you may feel complimented when you're called "grandma" or "granny." Lesley Stahl, the television anchor who gets most things right, even wrote a book about the joys of grandparenting.

She's stated publicly that everyone should be a grandma. No natural grandchildren? Go find some.

But some of us have no desire to be a grandma.

And when "grandma" (or even worse, "granny") is used as a placeholder for all older women, it's unlikely to evoke associations of a contemporary, educated professional who deserves respect.

Once you notice this trend, you see it everywhere.

Instead of writing, "When older people need more care," a journalist will write, "When Grandma needs more care ..."

An ad for a tech product: "So simple even Grandma could do it."

A group that rescues elderly dogs and cats: "The Grannies."

A website sharing discounts to people over 65: "Gift Card Granny" (The discounts aren't even that great.)

A home care agency near Philadelphia: "Granny's Helping Hand" (Don't let them near me.)

And the mother of them all, that awful song: "Grandma got run over by a reindeer."

For some reason it's funny when a little old lady gets killed by a runaway reindeer when she's walking along, minding her own business. Would it be funny with any other category?

In comedy routines, I ask the audience, "What if we substituted "little Asian boy" or "gorgeous gay dude" or "black teenager?"

Someone always goes, "Aww…"

And I say, "You didn't 'Aww' for the old lady."

To add insult to injury, the song claims she's determined to go out because she "forgot her medication." Of course, she's on meds: she's old.

Self-effacing Granny gets to heaven: "Saint Peter, you're telling me a reindeer put me up here? Well, it was my own fault. He's more important than I am. Hell, anybody's more important than I am. I must have been standing in his way."

Grandma As Drag Queen

Look up the "3 dancing English grannies" on YouTube. At first, I thought they were real kickass aging broads, making a statement about how older people can dance athletically. I was ready to be enthused.

Turns out they're actually frump-dressed young women. They wear gray wigs. The humor comes from, "It's funny because old people do it."

Why do we need these fakes? Just go on YouTube and you'll find women in their eighties and nineties doing everything from ballet to break dancing.

Let's try to imagine 3 white people putting on blackface and dancing.

Or 3 WASPs (White, Anglo-Saxon Protestants) putting on Jewish yarmulkes and dancing the hora as "the 3 Jews." Or three strong, athletic women hobbling onto the stage, waving crutches as if they were genuinely disabled.

The New York Times would run a dozen editorials and Twitter would come alive with "WTF" comments.

Don't let this one get away! Write some snarky comments on their YouTube channel.

"Old Face"

My friend was hunting down some props. His son's kindergarten was holding "old people's day." The kids, aged five, dressed up in "old people's clothes" with granny glasses.

Would they be allowed to dress up like "gay people?" Asians? Italians? Jews? Amish?

Could they limp around with a crutch as a disabled person?

Of course not. But this is "old face." No problem.

"Old people are funny."

I was talking to a well-meaning friend about my forays into open-mic standup comedy.

"Last time I killed it. I brought the house down. What a high."

My well-meaning friend smiled sweetly. "People will laugh just because you're old. It's funny to see an older person doing comedy."

I felt that sinking sensation in my stomach. I'd been so excited about my comedy success. She burst my bubble.

Comedy is tough. You sweat over your material. You practice. You can get a laugh -- or bomb with a thud -- just by changing a word or two, by changing the order of your bits, or by changing your timing.

And I've got news for you. People do not laugh at you just because you're old. Plenty of times I went up there, did my bits, and got nothing but a few bewildered looks. I've seen lots of "older" comics bomb at open mics. That sucks at any age.

Funny because I'm older? WTF?

You've probably noticed: everywhere you look, you'll find jokes about old people. "It's funny because you're old" really means, "It's funny because it's about old people." In other words, not funny.

Once you gain awareness, it's easy to tell the difference.

This joke is funny because it's not about being old. It's about the stupidity of government systems.

"I'm 80 so I'm exempt."
"You have to fill the forms out every year anyway."
"Why…do you think I'm getting younger?"

Demeaning: "You know you're old when your idea of happy hour is a nap."

Caricature: "As bland as Grandpa's salt-free dinner."

Just plain sick: This Postmates ad drew flak from social media: "When you want a whole cake to yourself because you're turning 30, Which is basically 50, which is basically dead."

In her book, *I Thought It Was Just Me,* Brene Brown identifies negative stereotypes of aging:

Despondent
Reclusive
Shrew/curmudgeon
Mildly impaired
Severely impaired
Vulnerable

The positive stereotypes aren't much better, Brown tells us. Who'd like to be a…

Happy and Active Golden Ager (who can be reduced to be a figure of fun)
Perfect Grandparent
Small Town Neighbor
John Wayne Conservative

These stereotypes "fit so closely that they give us permission to dismiss anything that deviates from that image," says Brene Brown.

And they give us permission to use ridicule and pretend we're just joking.

Brene Brown nails it when she points out that the "perfect grandma" knows her grandchildren are teasing when they say, "Dance for us, Grandma." The grandma does, although she feels hurt and shamed. They want to see her as a clown, not a whole person.

Frankly, that image gives me the creeps. Think of Nazi concentration camps where guards made prisoners "dance" by beating them. Think of scenes from the movie The Magdalen Sisters, where the nuns made their captives dance for their amusement. Think of dancing bears who are made to suffer to amuse an audience and make money for the circus.

"Don't trade self-respect for a laugh," says Brene Brown.

All too many people are willing to do just that. Just google "old people humor" on YouTube.

One of the most insidious YouTube videos features one Mary Maxwell, apparently a real person. At 72, she was invited to give the invocation at a convention of "Home Instead," an association of caregivers.

Ms. Maxwell gave a straightforward prayer, then turned back to the podium with a humorous line, "Just a minute, God, while I've got the microphone..."

So far, so good. Everybody laughed.

Ms. Maxwell proceeded to deliver a series of one-liners that recalled every stereotype in the book and then some. She leaves home with mismatched earrings. She leaves her left turn signal on all day. She pulls a shoulder-length chin hair. She drives up to a mailbox and orders a cheeseburger. She drives into a carwash the wrong way.

Frankly, 72 isn't that old. If she's got all these problems, it's not because she's old. She's got a neurological disorder.

Or she's just doing things people do at every age.

Once, on a business trip, I returned a rental car to the wrong agency. I handed over the keys and sprinted for my plane. I was twenty-six at the time.

Ms. Maxwell's audience loved her. She did, after all, bring a Miss Congeniality style to her talk: conservatively dressed, self-deprecating, gently humorous. She's not belting out jokes about sex toys like some comedians we know.

Thousands of people viewed this video. Sixty-five left comments. Sixty-three of those comments were positive. One of the other two was mine.

What's wrong with this gentle, very proper lady sharing some humor?

A lot, actually.

Thousands of YouTube viewers will remember the jokes. They'll remember Ms. Maxwell's age. A very large number of those listeners will forever associate "being in their seventies" with wearing mismatched earrings and driving into the wrong end of a carwash.

They don't stop to think, "It's comedy. Comedians exaggerate. They'll lie for a laugh."

And now a 72-year-old applies for a job or pitches a freelance gig.

What does the hiring manager remember? Oh yeah, that 70-something woman who kept getting all mixed up and losing things.

"We can't hire anyone who'd drive into the wrong end of a carwash," the manager says piously, writing a big red X on the over-65 applications.

In 2021, the US President was 78 years old, he's not showing any signs of slowing down. Yet we still saw snarky comments about his age in the comment sections of social media.

In 1998, the snark was more obvious when astronaut John Glenn returned to space as a 77-year-old. Apparently, NASA wanted to study the effects of space travel on older people.

The media fixated firmly – and solely – on his age. A *New York Times* article ran with the title, "Space Aged".

"On February 20, 1962," they reported, "John Glenn flew over a country with 80 million fewer people than it has today, a land without ZIP codes and throughout which three-quarters of the households still contained both husbands and wives."

Of course, some things don't change. The same article referred to "dismaying" editorials and added, "Jay Leno said there would be no spacewalk on STS-95 because NASA feared Glenn might 'wander off.'"

An article claiming to be scholarly analyzed media references to Glenn's mission, claiming to find "few" instances of ageism. Yet in just the half dozen or so articles they studied, all from major news magazines, they quoted lines like, "the old man had a lot to learn." One article references the skills he'd need to master "at an age when most Americans have long since retired."

Apparently "long since retired" means "dead in the brain." We'll come back to this when we talk about retirement as the R-word.

Forget the reindeer. The real Grandma got run over by the stereotypes.

Stereotypes can kill. They'll kill you faster if you try to be a good sport about it.

Quoted in Next Avenue, author Steve Petrow writes:

"I have friends who send me these memes that they think are funny, but they're mean. I got one last week: his grandma unfriended someone on Facebook, then the image is a phone and she's got her white-out out and she's painting over his name.

"But when someone in my generation is propagating that, it comes across as this is acceptable to make fun of each other. But it's kind of insidious. And internalized ageism, especially, leads to greater rates of physical disease, mental health diagnosis and a shorter life span."

A study of veterans found that those who resisted stereotyping were less likely to consider suicide, experience anxiety, or report symptoms of post-traumatic stress disorder (PTSD).

A *New York Times* article summarizes research showing that older adults who internalize stereotypes - accepting their role as silly and incompetent - can experience "poorer mental and physical health."

That's a high price to pay, just to get a laugh.

Stereotypes kill because they replace youth primes with old primes.

Bruce Grierson gained considerable insight into aging when he wrote *What Makes Olga Run*, the book about a woman who began track and field at 77 and continued till she died suddenly at 95.

Speaking at a Ted Talk, Grierson refers to "youth primes" - cues in the environment that prompt us to feel young. Olga was exposed to a youth prime every time she showed up for a track and field event.

Of course, the classic example is the Ellen Langer experiment we discussed in Chapter 1, where men in their 70s were put into a time warp and invited to return to their younger days.

Stereotypes replace youth primes with age primes. I get this when I'm caught up in a workout at the gym.

For me, the gym acts as a youth prime. I've been working out in gyms since my twenties.

Then someone comes along to say, "I want to be like you when I get older." They intend to be complimentary, but they just introduced a new prime. I'm no longer just another person working out. I'm a frail little old lady. And I'm furious.

To overcome the stereotypes, you have to do two things.

First, you have to risk being rejected.

You don't have to come from a position of anger and attack. You can start out nice. But you have to risk hearing, "I thought she was such a nice old lady. She's really a *bitch*."

Second, you have to fight against "what everybody knows."

People take a lot of things for granted when it comes to aging. They assume as you get older, you'll get weaker, sicker, and less mentally alert. They assume you aren't working or working out. You certainly aren't holding your own in a Zumba class.

You don't have to settle for being Miss Congeniality. You can refuse to participate in any program where you have a possibility of being treated as a second-rate person. You can speak up when anyone — even (or especially) when a medical professional says, "At your age..." You can flip someone the bird when they call you "grandma." Even better, retaliate by calling them a "silly little prick" or yes, even a "motherfucking asshole."

Just do it in a way that won't get you arrested. In most countries going to jail is the one thing you're never too old to do.

Chapter 3: "Call me honey and I'll call you a motherfucking idiot"

Imagine you walk into a diner, sit down on a stool at the counter, order your coffee, turn to your left and see Willie Nelson - the iconic 80-something country music artist - occupying the next seat. What would you say?

Would you ask him about writing "On the Road Again" on the back of an airline barf bag? Would you tell him that "Angel Flying Too Close to the Ground" makes you cry every time?

Or something like this: "Oooh, Mr. Nelson, let's be careful with our coffee now, sweetie. Is that hot? Is it HOTTT?"

Now imagine Willie punching you right in the face.

Cynthia Dampier in the *Chicago Tribune*.

Miss Congeniality Grandma doesn't swear. She does a little hissy frown when someone swears in front of her.

She's also not real.

Google "old people swearing." What comes up? Articles about dementia patients who swear. Talk to a *real* person over sixty and you'll get an earful.

These days, most people swear. So the subtext is, "You're not a real person if you're old. If you do things most people do, you're odd."

Personally, I believe swearing is a skill you need to master as you age. It's the only way to respond to the idiots you'll encounter who are determined to treat you like a five-year-old.

Treating older people like children isn't just insensitive it's cruel.

John Leland sums it up perfectly in a New York Times article:

"Professionals call it elderspeak, the sweetly belittling form of address that has always rankled older people: the doctor who talks to their child rather than to them about their health; the store clerk who assumes that an older person does not know how to work a computer, or needs to be addressed slowly or in a loud voice. Then there are those who address any elderly person as 'dear…'

Leland even points to research showing that patients become more aggressive and less cooperative when subjected to "elderspeak."

Seems reasonable to me. Why cooperate with someone who treats you in an insulting, demeaning manner? Often you won't get their attention unless you swear at them.

Elderspeak has been recognized with its own page on Wikipedia [emphasis added]:

"Elderspeak is a specialized speech style used by younger adults with older adults, characterized by simpler vocabulary and sentence structure, filler words, lexical fillers, overly-endearing terms, closed-ended questions, using the collective "we", repetition, and speaking more slowly...Although some aspects of elderspeak may be beneficial for some recipients, it is generally seen as inappropriate and a hindrance to intergenerational communication."

Writing in PsychCentral, the blog of *Psychology Today*, journalist Susan Hooper pointed out that being called "hon" or "dear" meant she wasn't being taken seriously. And as she got older, she heard those terms more and more.

Hooper adds, almost apologetically,

"It may seem foolish to get upset over the inappropriate use of a term of endearment when there are people facing physical danger every day because of the color of their skin, their ancestry, the place where they worship, the gender of their partner or even the way they pronounce English."

It is hard to imagine anyone apologizing for getting angry over inappropriate terms related to race, religion, disability, or sexual orientation. It's even harder to imagine readers dismissing these concerns, as many of the 70 commenters did.

The best way to respond to someone who talks down to you? Practice swearing.

In his earlier *New York Times* article, John Leland interviewed Ellen Kirschman, then aged 68, a police psychologist in Northern California. Ms. Kirschman objected to people calling her "young lady," which she called "mocking and disingenuous...As I get older, I don't want to be recognized for my age. I want to be recognized for my accomplishments, for my wisdom."

To avoid stereotyping, Ms. Kirschman said, she "often sprinkles her conversation with profanities" when she is among people who do not know her. "That makes them think, 'This is someone to be reckoned with,'" she said. "A little sharpness seems to help."

Swearing solves most of your other problems as well.

For instance, sooner or later you'll tangle with an insurance company. You'll be talking to some poorly trained representative who's getting rewarded for getting rid of you. Swearing is the "open sesame" to getting in front of someone who can actually help.

Before I got a decent insurance plan, I once got into a heated discussion with a rep who kept saying, "You need to have a preferred provider." In a tone more suited to talking to a ten-year-old, she said, "Let me explain what preferred provider means…"

After going a few unproductive rounds with this unhelpful rep, I finally said: "Listen, you motherfucking idiot, I know what a preferred provider is! I'm trying to figure out if this particular provider is covered."

She didn't hang up on me. She said politely, with new respect, "I'll get back to you." An hour later she called back, very humbly, with all my questions answered.

For those of you saying, "You can catch more flies with honey," I'm here to say, "That doesn't work with insurance companies. Give an insurance company honey and they'll put it on their French toast and charge you for an out-of-network breakfast."

I do miss the old-fashioned swear words, like "gosh darn." I love saying things like "He's a pain in the patootie."

Today nobody gets it. Patooties aren't funny anymore. You have to use the "a" word. So lean in and learn a few.

Swearing will change the way people see you. Get ready to hear, "But I thought you were such a nice old lady." Or even, "Boy, she's really a bitch, isn't she?"

Well, yes, that's exactly the point.

It's been a while since swearing made women blush.

As I'm writing this, in the first quarter of the twenty-first century, many men still apologize for swearing in front of women, especially older women. They're confusing cohort effects with aging effects: your great-grandmother was brought up to believe that nice ladies didn't smoke or swear (or at least they didn't admit it).

Your baby boomer grandma grew up swearing and hasn't looked back.

Sometimes this old-fashioned super-politeness gets super-ridiculous.

One night I'd finished my set at an open mic in a comedy club. I was standing outside talking to some male comics. One used the word "fucking" and then turned to me to apologize: "Excuse me, ma'am."

Ignoring the ma'am, I asked him, "Did you just hear me when I was up on that stage? I was using some pretty choice words myself."

Another time I was invited to be in a comedy show...for the wrong reason. The first part of the show had the audience going around to different stations and doing something that would be funny. The organizer had come across a book of insults.

For my station, he thought it would be funny for people to insult an old person. Guess who'd be the "old person."

Fortunately, the invitation came by email so I had time to calm down after processing the double insult -- that I was so obviously "old" and that older people couldn't be insulted. Believe me, five minutes in a medical setting will demonstrate that lots of people think it's perfectly proper to deliver withering insults to older people.

Instead, I suggested, I could dress up as a nun. The Swearing Nun. Delivering insults to a nun would be funny. After all, we're in Philadelphia, where many adults still have vivid memories of old-time Catholic schools with ruler-wielding nuns.

And so I did.

One of the guys lent me a Halloween costume. People came up and read insults. I gave them the finger, made vague motions that could be interpreted as blessings or threats, and glared at them. A few people murmured, "I couldn't say that to a nun!"

When this portion of the show was over, the MC announced, "Sister Deborah, did you have any final words for our audience?"

I came out, glared at everybody, and said, "Yes! I have a special dispensation to call you all a bunch of motherfucking assholes."

That line brought down the house. It was one of my happiest comedy moments. And my language has continued to deteriorate ever since.

If you're having trouble saying the words, take a stand-up comedy workshop.

As one friend says, "Let your inner frat boy come out." You'll be better equipped to deal with the world as you age. It is curiously liberating to call a roomful of adults "motherfucking assholes" and not only get away with it, but also get a hearty round of applause.

Chapter 4: Playing the age card: Miss Congeniality Grandma turns the tables (and sometimes throws them).

"The greatest trick the Devil ever pulled was convincing the world he didn't exist"—Charles Baudelaire (and others).

Did you see the movie *The Usual Suspects*? Can you ever forget the moment we figure out who's the powerful Kayzer Sose? That's what playing the age card feels like.

For one sweet moment, Miss Congeniality Grandma gets her revenge.

Soothed by the stereotypes, they patronize you. They figure you'll be an easy mark. So you play "helpless old lady."

It works every time.

When I googled "playing the age card," I found stories about people talking their way out of traffic tickets and getting to the head of the line because they're old.

I once read about a woman who walks five miles a day but shows up at the airport with a cane. Limping to the check-in desk, she asks for a wheelchair and gets early boarding.

My rule is, if someone treats me like an old lady, I'll usually play along. When the bus comes, everyone usually waits for me to go on first. I've learned to move quickly so we don't spend fifteen minutes begging each other to go ahead.

 If someone holds a door, I'll thank them … and I hold doors for anyone of any age, male or female, if they've got their hands full.

Sometimes the stereotypes will put an age card right in your hand.

When I showed up for my first Covid shot, the volunteer staffer asked me earnestly, "Will you be able to stand in line? Do you need a wheelchair?"

"Will that get me to the head of the line faster?" I asked, eyeing the file of vaccination wannabes stretched around the block.

"Absolutely!" she said.

I was *so* tempted.

But I felt guilty.

"I do Zumba workouts twice a week," I said. "Do I still qualify?"

She assured me I would. Age trumps everything in the medical world.

I couldn't bring myself to do it. Fortunately, the line moved really fast.

But sometimes I've given in…

One time I was crossing a street in snowy weather. I was trying to figure out how to jump over the ice when a well-meaning young man asked, "Do you need some help?"

"You bet!" I said, grabbing his arm. "And could you carry my backpack too?"

"Sure," he said kindly. And he walked me a whole block to the door of my gym, where I thanked him profusely, shouldered my backpack, and climbed a steep flight of stairs to my weight training class.

And this one would have been tempting …

I laughed out loud when I read this note in the "comments" section of a New York Times article:

"I am 80 and it's a pretty darn good age to be; I remain active; work part-time, play tennis, teach at a local college. But some days, the impact of the 'structural ageism' described here is overwhelming… Last week, checking out at the grocery store, a young man behind me tapped me on the shoulder and said, 'I want to pay for your groceries.'"

Ah, what an opportunity to play the age card.

"Can you wait a minute? I'm going back to add some steaks and seafood, as long as you're buying."

Serious Age Game Players

Christiane Northrup, the author of *Goddesses Never Age*, rejects the age card. She recommends turning down senior discounts because they're constant reminders of being "old."

In psychological terms, your discount card would be called a "prime." Earlier I talked about the "age primes" and "youth primes" Bruce Grierson described in his Ted Talk.

For instance, when women are primed with reminders of being female, they perform less effectively on a math test. Similarly, every time you use a senior discount card, you're reminded that you're beyond a certain age; you might live up to the ageist stereotypes by moving more slowly or becoming more forgetful.

Christiane Northrup has a point. Using a senior pass does force me to remember I'm old.

On the other hand, a senior pass or discount feels like something I've earned as well as payback for age discrimination that denies me access to jobs. I feel more like a VIP when I flash my pass and hop on a bus...especially in summer, when I'm wearing gym shorts and a tee.

During the early pandemic, I almost felt guilty when I shopped at the farmer's market during "senior hours." I walked over a mile to get there and usually walked home, carrying my healthy, heavy items in my trusty backpack.

As it happened, I usually arrived too late to qualify for early shopping anyway.

Getting Carded: NOT playing the Age Card

For a long time now, I haven't bothered carrying an ID. When I go into a bar, the bouncers look right past me.

But when you google "getting carded at age 60" or "getting carded at 70," a lot of stories come up. Apparently, some places believe they're required to card everyone. You'll find stories of eighty-year-olds who couldn't buy a beer because they never thought to bring ID.

Nobody -- absolutely nobody -- gets flattered when they get carded at an advanced age. They know there's no way you look twenty-one, let alone eighteen. Getting carded in your seventies feels insulting, not flattering.

And pretty much everyone agrees, it's not a big deal...except it's annoying if. they look you straight in your post-cataract eye and say, "Sorry, you can't have that glass of wine."

Frankly, I'm with the folks who walked out when some young teenager asked for their ID to buy a drink. There are plenty of places to drink where they'll respect your obvious maturity.

I must admit I sometimes wished I'd get carded on Amtrak while traveling at the senior rate. That never happened. Must be the frizzy hair...or else a lot of conductors are too old to be fooled.

But if you want to start enjoying senior rates somewhere, start with movie theatres. The first time, I said diffidently, "I believe I qualify for the senior discount." An older male friend snorted. "Just put your money down and say, 'One. Senior.'"

To be fair, the pimply young kid working the movie theatre would give you a pass when you're twenty-five. Anyone who's graduated high school seems impossibly old.

The REALLY Fun Part of Playing the Age Card

For a female, the best part of playing the age card comes when you want to hang out with a younger male. I've always wanted a brother, so I like being around guys when I get to be the big sister. I like having coffee or lunch. But a surprising number of guys -- not just former VP Pence -- have hang-ups about eating dinner with a woman.

A less surprising number of their wives have even more hang-ups.

When I was younger, I'd often want to join a male colleague for lunch or even dinner, if we were traveling. When I'd meet his wife, she'd give me that look married women give single women: "Keep your goddam paws off my husband."

And I'd return the look with one of my own: "Honey, your husband has all the sex appeal of an earthworm. Just because I enjoy being with him in the coffee shop doesn't mean I want to join him in the bedroom."

Once you reach a certain age, that stops. Everybody figures he's your nephew.

The movie, *My Afternoons with Marguerite*, gives us a beautiful example. Marguerite, a highly educated, book-loving 95-year-old woman, befriends Germain, who's got a reputation as the village idiot. Their relationship becomes mutually respectful and mutually nurturing. They discover they're soulmates, in one of those quirky friendships that can go really deep.

Because she's 95, Germain's girlfriend isn't the least bit jealous; she even encourages him to read to Marguerite when Marguerite's eyesight begins to fail. If Marguerite had been closer to Germain's age, the whole scene would have been different.

The Best Age Card Player award goes to Willie Murphy.

You've probably heard this story.

On November 22, 2019, a man tried to open the door to Willie Murphy's home, pleading, "I need money for food." She told him to go away.

Fooled by the voice of an aging female, the man broke in … only to discover Willie Murphy, age 82, a female bodybuilder who can deadlift 250 pounds. She picked up a table, threw it at him, and then really went to work. By the time the cops came, he was just as glad to see them as she was.

That's the ultimate way to play the age card. Don't just turn the tables. Throw them.

Funny… absolutely nobody said Willie Murphy was "cute."

Chapter 5:
"Don't send me to prison and call it a party"

"It is a sad commentary that some elderly people would be better off committing a felony such as counterfeiting money; in prison, their assets are preserved, their meals are guaranteed, and their health care is scrupulously monitored and fully covered." - Nortin Hadler, Rethinking Aging. pp 171-172.

When people cling to the stereotypes, they get to avoid thinking of older people as real. Miss Congeniality Grandma smiles cheerfully as she's led away to her nursing home. She'll make the best of everything. After all, she figures, she doesn't deserve more.

An aging broad, who doesn't mind being called a bitch, feels differently. She wants the option to take a cyanide pill along with her cup of chamomile tea.

That's a purely rational decision.

During World War II, spies knew they were taking a risk. If captured, they'd be tortured and then killed.

They held on to their cyanide pills. Death was better than torture. Everyone knew that. You didn't need to see a psychiatrist. If you'd rather die before torture than after, you were indisputably sane.

It's not a legend. Madeleine Albright's book, *Prague Winter*, describes a woman who'd obtained cyanide from the underground resistance movement. When the German soldiers prepared to torture her, she asked for a moment to go to the bathroom. She popped her pill and died immediately.

Sure, it was painful. But compared to her son, who died after hours of physical and mental torture, she got a cakewalk.

If I ran the world, we would be eligible for a cyanide pill at the same time we become eligible for Medicare.

You wouldn't have to take it. But you could.

And, like the spies in World War II, you shouldn't need a psychiatrist to decide if you were "normal." If you're forced to eject from a fighter plane and you know you're facing torture in an enemy POW camp, nobody thinks you're crazy if you reach for your pill.

Why should you be considered crazy if you want to avoid torture while you lie helpless in an overpriced, under-regulated "care" facility?

If you take too long to die, you'll end up in a prison.

If you become helpless as you age, sooner or later you'll end up in that "facility," unless you have incredibly devoted relatives who have space, patience, and skill to care for you.

The facility might be fairly benign. You might have your own apartment and eat meals in a lovely dining room...until you become helpless. Then you're at the mercy of whoever's desperate enough to hold a job there.

Many articles refer to the need to "convince your parents to move to assisted living." This article is typical:

"Seniors can thrive [in assisted living] for several reasons. ALFs [Assisted Living Facilities] have trained staff around 24/7 in case residents need medical help or other assistance. Fully prepared nutritious food and snacks are available. Perhaps, most importantly, seniors can make new friends and have an abundance of engaging activities to choose from."

What they're NOT saying is, you can't refuse that 24/7 medical care and opt to die instead. That "nutritious food" is probably bland and, like any institutional food, repetitive.

Want to say, "To hell with my diet – I want to live now?" That well-meaning staff will insist your life is still worth living when the treat of the week consists of a few stalks of overcooked broccoli.

Your opportunities to "make new friends" will be limited to your fellow inmates, all of a similar age and degree of helplessness, mostly female. You may or may not have something in common with them. You might even be forced to share with a cellmate who snores or talks nonstop.

True, you have no household responsibilities...but you also don't engage in meaningful activities that challenge your intellect and help you grow out of your comfort zone.

Worst of all, you're supposed to forget that you're paying for this. You pay a high price if you refuse your Miss Congeniality role.

Too bitchy? You'll get booted to a state institution where you'll be tied to a wheelchair in front of a television set, with no bathroom breaks, no privacy, and plenty of meds with horrendous side effects.

Some people love communal living.

For them, it's a long cruise on a ship that doesn't move. They thrive on group activities and enjoy the people. They also have relatives who are willing and able to advocate for them *and* who have standing to sue.

In her book, *No Stopping Us Now: The Adventures of Older Women in American History*, Gail Collins points out that "we" now have many options for living arrangements as "we" age. (She also notes that these options multiply as you get wealthier.)

One facility has a four-year waiting list, Collins says. "They're engaged in all sorts of group projects, from counseling undocumented immigrants in nearby communities to holiday entertainments," she writes.

For one holiday project, residents celebrated the 4th of July by voting on what the national anthem should be. "This land is your land" got way ahead of the current Star-Spangled Banner.

Be still, my beating heart.

Even Gail Collins admits, "There does seem to be something about cruise ships that sends certain people over the edge."

That would be me.

Active living is a picnic compared to assisted living and nursing homes.

Some of the elderly in Japan apparently figured this out. "Aging outlaws" are committing crimes to get into prison because they have nowhere else to go. "Life inside is never easy," says the reporter, "but life outside is worse."

Eighteen percent of Japanese inmates (20% of the female inmates) are over 60. Crimes by the elderly have quadrupled in the past 20 years. One-third of those released end up back inside. It costs $20,000 a year to keep someone in prison, not to mention medical expenses. Unlike nursing homes, prisons don't have waiting lists.

Some people, especially women, value the companionship they won't find on the outside. Even working in the prison factory offers a more productive way to spend time than what they could get in a typical nursing home.

Prisons and nursing homes have a lot in common...

...arbitrary rules, treating residents as inmates rather than consumers, punishing complainers, and serving bad food.

Just google "restraint chairs in prisons." Prisons can tie inmates to chairs for days at a time, without breaks for bathrooms or meals. Cruel and unusual? It's not unusual for understaffed nursing homes to park residents in wheelchairs in front of a television set for hours at a time, wearing diapers.

In his book, *What Doctors Won't Tell You About Getting Older*, geriatrician Mark Lachs shares a horror story. He was consulted by relatives of an elderly female nursing home patient. She suffered from severe diabetes and dementia. The nursing home staff stuck needles in her arm for blood tests several times a day. Sometimes they even plunged needles into her abdomen. The woman's nephew begged Dr. Lachs to intervene.

This woman didn't know why they were sticking her with needles and neither did Dr. Lachs. Blindness was not a concern: she hadn't been able to read in years because her brain scrambled her eyesight

The nursing home applied a regimen that might be suitable for a forty-year-old without dementia. The nursing home doctor - fresh out of residency - refused Dr. Lachs's intervention. It wasn't clear what could be done to save this woman. Her torture might have a place in a concentration camp.

When you can't leave a place voluntarily, you're a captive.

Paula Span, writing in *The New York Times*, reported the "benefits" experienced by those living in retirement communities and nursing homes —" the very destinations so many people dread. They can provide proximity, shared activities, and a larger pool of prospective friends."

She visits Hebrew Home for the Aged, which is one of the more expensive homes. She talks to a few outgoing people and claims people in homes manage to avoid loneliness. They've dreaded going to this place, she says, and they're not miserable after all.

That's the same message John Leland shares in his book, *Happiness Is a Choice You Make*. A woman develops a relationship with a fellow inmate and then they're separated. So what? She's adaptable. She adjusts. See, old age means resilience, the book seems to suggest. The problem isn't the nursing homes; it's the attitude of the residents.

But we're seeing just the tip of the iceberg. Twenty to forty percent of people in nursing homes have been abused...and that estimate is probably low. A survey of four thousand nursing home assistants found that abuse in these settings occurred on an everyday basis.

A report published by the National Research Council provides a horrifying catalog of abuses. They note that one Georgia study found 44% of residents surveyed reported abuse. There's no way to measure abuse accurately.

"When I told the nursing home staff I was taking my terminally ill mother out for ice cream," a friend says, "the staff warned me, 'Don't spoil her appetite for dinner.'"

As a certified bitchy broad, I would argue that depriving someone of ice cream should be prosecuted as criminal conduct … especially if it's creamy coffee ice cream with a dollop of sinful hot fudge. By the time you've passed seventy-five, you won't lose a day of longevity if you enjoy every delicious morsel.

To avoid ending up in miserable nursing homes, we're urged to "make plans."

What kind of a plan can you make? Maybe you've got long-term care insurance, but who's going to make sure your caregivers don't steal from you and abuse you?

Who's going to visit you when you're locked up in a prison-like institution? How can you avoid being stuck in a wheelchair in front of a television all day? Who's going to negotiate with an insurance company when they decide you don't qualify for payment? Who's going to be sure you're fed, taken to the bathroom, and treated with dignity?

Personally, I wonder who's going to fight for me when I've been drugged up because I dared to question the petty authority of my guardians. Residents who resist care are most likely to be subject to abuse, which can include kicking and hitting. Suffering in silence has never been one of my virtues.

Can we reform nursing homes?

We have a better chance of reforming the prisons. At least in theory the inmates have access to lawyers. Unlike many nursing home residents, most prisoners are capable of speaking and writing. Some of them even get released. I suspect prison guards earn a lot more than nursing home caregivers and for sure they've got a stronger union.

But ask any criminal defense lawyer, especially one who practices federal white-collar crime: "Do you think the system can change?"

They'll say no. And they're highly paid, high-profile lawyers – as powerful as you can get.

Every year, mainstream news outlets (think *New York Times*) publish articles decrying the plight of people in nursing homes. Problems were highlighted even more during the pandemic. Nothing has happened: owners are motivated by economic rewards and governments are muzzled by lobbyists.

Optimists point to the Green House project - a plan to create homes, each occupied by ten people living in private rooms. The homes cost more but have been shown to slash medical costs and achieve high survival rates during the pandemic. Currently about 300 homes exist for about 3200 residents - a drop in the bucket.

Options for creating these homes on a larger scale seem to be under discussion. However, as more homes come into existence, you would need to expand the labor pool of aides. It's too early to tell how this model will impact care for the majority of elders in the US.

Barry Berman, a nursing home owner and executive, extensively researched options after his own mother declined quickly in a nursing home he ran. Attempting to emulate the Green House model, Berman found they could create quality environments, but couldn't scale to meet the demand.

Worse, the "economics" forced them to put two people in a room - a situation that many of us would see as worse than death.

More and more people are living alone. If you haven't shared a home in forty or fifty years, you're unlikely to function happily when you have to share a room.

More significantly, nursing homes are lightly regulated and heavily protected. During Covid, few nursing home executives were held accountable for deaths and disease among their residents.

"The industry, with its powerful lobby, has escaped significant scrutiny," writes Matthew Cunningham-Cook in The Intercept. "Just two nursing home executives have been indicted for Covid-19 deaths, while the industry showered over $10 million on candidates and political action committees in 2020, according to data collected by the National Institute on Money in Politics.

Charlene Harrington, professor emerita of Social Behavioral Sciences at the University of California, San Francisco, says 70% of nursing homes are for-profit and low staffing is common.

"They're trying to make money," she says. "And the main way to make money is to keep labor costs low."

The sheer cruelty of the nursing home model - making money from the most helpless people on the planet - should make us think of concentration camps, where inmates were forced to labor to the point of death, denied food, and robbed of their possessions.

When we recognize these "care communities" as prisons, we will respect those who'd literally die to escape.

After all, they've committed no crime except to live beyond their ability to take care of themselves. I don't see any way to improve conditions in the US, given our political model that supports lobbying and a belief that market forces will lead to change.

Beyond politics, we know that potential child abusers often seek out jobs as coaches and teachers. It's likely that people who secretly hate their elders will seek out jobs in care homes, looking for opportunities for abuse.

Well-meaning reformers can't make the numbers work. The only way to effect change is to allow voluntary exit through assisted dying. And that's the next chapter.

Chapter 6: "Assisted living can be more painful than assisted dying."

"For us, it was never about death. It was about life. Knowing that there was a way out, and that his suffering was not going to become unendurable, was the one thing that allowed Mr. Peterson to go on living, much longer than he would have otherwise wanted." Gavin Extence, *The Universe Versus Alex Woods*

In her book, *Never Say Die*, Susan Jacoby shares an unforgettable story.

An elderly man was forced to replace "living alone" with "living with a caretaker." He was miserable. One day he stole the caretaker's car keys, drove to the nearest bridge, and jumped.

It's not suicide, says Jacoby. It's a rational choice. He shouldn't have been forced to jump off a bridge. Some people would have been happy with his life, but he wasn't. He was ready to go. No amount of therapy or medications could change him.

Quoted by Jane Brody in *The New York Times*, Gregory Brown (described as a "suicide specialist" at University of Pennsylvania) "recommended that older adults structure their days by maintaining a regular cycle and planning activities that 'give them pleasure, purpose and a reason for living.'"

Frankly, that comes across as insensitive. What if you're physically unable to do anything that gives you "pleasure, purpose and a reason for living?"

Sometimes you just don't want to keep going. You're ready for the Final Exit.

I've been on many long, cross-country drives. And I know how it feels to be ready to arrive at your destination realizing you just don't have the energy to go much further.

You're so tired you have to force yourself to stay awake. All you can think of is finding your exit and looking for your motel in the dark, and you hope like hell they didn't lose your reservation.

You see signs, "Last exit in Nowheresville." If you miss that exit, you'll be driving for a while.

You know you're ready to stop. They want you to keep going.

When you're in a hospital or "care facility," you could reach a point when you're ready to stop. There's no point in going on. You won't make it to the next town. You want to grab that last exit. Of course, the kindly medical people want to keep you on the road, half-zonked and wholly miserable. You're ready to take that exit and never get back on the road again.

The author of *The Longevity Economy*, who gets a lot of stuff right, missed this one. People say they want to die, he says, but the story changes when you see people in emergency rooms. Now they're demanding a full court press on healing.

Ashton Applewhite, in *This Chair Rocks*, also points out that we can't always predict our reactions when faced with imminent death. She quotes a geriatrician, Dr. Thomas Finucane of Johns Hopkins, who repeats a Mexican saying: "The bull looks different when you enter the ring." Many people change their minds about enforcing a DNR when they're actually in the medical setting, he says.

Katy Butler, author of *Knocking on Heaven's Door*, provides a more nuanced and also more horrific view. In one hospital, bioethicist Katrina Bramstedt "functioned somewhat like an informal judge... the arbiter when a family like mine found itself unexpectedly powerless in the face of advanced medicine." (p, 155). A fifth of American deaths take place in intensive care, "where ten days of futile flailing can cost as much as $325,000." (p. 5)

ER doctors have been known to follow procedures first and ask questions later. Nobody knows how many of those "give me everything!" people were responding to exaggerated promises.

I can just hear that doc saying, "If we do this, you'll stay alive and be back to work in no time. If we don't, you'll die."

In fact, Katy Butler's mother negotiated with a doctor who was determined to perform a heart operation. Acknowledging the risk of stroke, the doctor bargained: "Just a little weakness on one side?"

That's like the Mafia bargaining with someone who welshed on their debt: "We'll cut off just one finger…"

"Too much temptation for the family?"

Then there's the argument, "If we legalized assisted dying, your family could bump you off."

My answer is, "If they want to get rid of you, they'll make your life miserable anyway. And they will let you die from neglect, much more painfully."

Katy Butler expresses this point forcefully (p 270):

"Anyone who attempts to open a public conversation about rehumanizing modern death must be prepared to weather charges of medical rationing, promoting 'death panels,' canonizing Dr. Kevorkian, and discriminating against the aged, demented or disabled.

"The word 'rationing' avoids the reality that our current way of dying maximizes both cost and suffering. The phrase 'death panels' glosses over the fact that the mortality rate remains at 100 percent. Vilifying Dr. Kevorkian ignores the problem that many saw him as solving: the loss of autonomy near the end of life to medical overdoing."

What about hospice? Evan Boudreau, in his article for Canadian Catholic register, promises a "Hospice to provide safe haven from euthanasia for patients and doctors."

Hospices aren't always hospitable.

Boudreau describes a 10-room hospice with "pull-out sofas for loved ones." Patients get "medication to alleviate suffering, meals and people for social comfort."

I'm perfectly fine with this option. But it's an expensive solution for just ten people, who must come fully equipped with "loved ones."

The reality is that medication, which often comes with horrific side effects, doesn't guarantee pain relief. The most benevolent pain meds can make people so sleepy, they remain in their beds in a comatose state, with zero quality of life, too weak to resist abuse.

Some pain can't be fixed, even with medication. Nobody's telling you about people screaming in pain from their hospice beds.

With just 10 residents and a dedicated religion-based staff, the meals might be better than palatable. As for "social comfort," you need to ask the single, never-married people with no close family members.

Personally, I won't derive a lot of comfort from a stranger who's paid to be kind or who's volunteered to hold my hand at my bedside. It's like getting sex for money. I'd rather cuddle up with a cat.

Some doctors are beginning to recognize the reality.

In his book *The Wonder of Aging*, Michael Gurian quotes his friend Lloyd Halpern:

"If Alzheimer's strikes me, I [hope I would] have the wisdom to take my own life in a planned, serene ceremony with my family there at my side. I wanted to be able to say goodbye to my family, and them to me, with meaning and understanding. I wanted to teach my children that death is a part of life, and that dying with dignity is a choice we can all make." (Pp 256-257)

Gurian refers to this approach as "completion spirituality," i.e., we are hardwired as a species to protect those who love us.

"If we come to feel that our illness is destroying that legacy-- destroying its memories, invading our family's good life, destroying our children's inheritance -- it is natural for us to want to end our lives to provide for our family and protect our family from years of suffering." (p 256)

Lloyd Halpern (as quoted by Gurian) points out that in every culture, we honor those who sacrifice themselves for others. We do this in war. So why not in old age?

Gurian (p 258) proposes the "three conversations rule:" if a person expresses a wish to die in three conversations over three months, then that wish should be honored."

He also points out that the legal system creates obstacles to honoring our end-of-life wishes. In Washington State, you're allowed access to assisted dying. But you can't get assisted dying in a hospital. And if you want to donate your organs, you must die in a hospital. So, if you want to donate your much-needed organs, you must prolong your death.

In today's world, you aren't always protected by a DNR or advance directive. Somebody's got to be there advocating for you -- and in some cases, advocating pretty aggressively. It's not enough to have that paper in your file. Your designated medical proxy is on vacation in Bali and you're in New York? Too bad for you.

Here's my proposal for achieving a comfortable End of Life.

First, you get to record your DNR as a tattoo or bracelet. Why should you need an in-person proxy when someone can link to your digital records? The IRS already has records of our past lives: you'll be asked to remember where you lived twenty years ago when you're claiming your tax refund. A tattoo could be a URL or a QR code linked to your living will.

The day you become eligible for Medicare, you would be allowed to request your very own cyanide pill, to use as you like, whenever you like, no questions asked.

You would also be offered a gift certificate to a hit man in the nearest Mafia enclave. It's quick and final.

And for a little extra cash, your death will get written up as an accident or unsolved murder. For those who worry about their family's guilt, this solution works perfectly.

Have you noticed that all these namby-pamby, cheery-chirp-up books about aging tiptoe around the subject?

Some articles insist that older people claim they want to die because they're just depressed. With just a dash of therapy and a few pills, they'll be eager to live a meaningless life, in constant pain, eating bad food, no privacy, unable to read or watch movies, attended by low-paid employees whose attitudes range from indifference to outright cruelty.

Sorry, folks, that's not depression. That's a case of "Give me liberty or give me death." Why does Patrick Henry get to be a hero when he says it, while an older person gets labeled "depressed?"

Why did spy pilots get to evade capture and torture without seeing a psychiatrist on their way down?

Let's allow people to get off the highway when they're too tired to drive anymore.

A Prisoner of Your Own Body

In *What Makes Olga Run*, journalist Bruce Grierson tells the story of a 90-year-old woman who was winning marathons. Grierson wrote this book seeking answers to the question "Why is this woman functioning at a high level when others in her age group are barely functioning, if they're alive?"

At one point, the author's sister asks their grandmother, "What does it feel like to be 100?" The grandmother replies, "I hope you never find out."

The woman's mind was "sharp as Cheddar," but she was "essentially body-locked...like a transcendently beautiful butterfly pinned to a board. She died -- was released, really -- just shy of 102."

Even more publicly, Australian scientist David Goodall turned 104 in May of 2018. When asked if he'd had a nice birthday, he told the Australian Broadcasting Corporation, "No, I'm not happy. I want to die...It's not sad, really. What is sad is if one is prevented." He was off to Switzerland for legally assisted dying.

"I don't want to be a burden..."

Let's face it: you're going to be a burden to someone if you end up with one of those diseases where you suffer for years and need endless care. You can't open a newspaper without reading about the challenges of caretaking.

Caregiving can be described as a "Roller-Coaster Ride from Hell," according to Jane Brody of *The New York Times*. You can't get more direct than that.

The truth is, after a few months under the care of a caretaker, you'll be remembered as a nuisance. You're no longer the love of someone's life. And if they're honest, most caretakers will admit, they're relieved to see you go.

The readers' comments are even more helpful than the article.

"I realize that caregivers need to band together to advocate for a euthanasia pill. No one really wants to take care of disabled relatives. Why not be honest about it? Do you think that the person you care for doesn't know how you feel? If I had access to a death pill, I'd take it before this day was out."

Some compared caregiving to being under "house arrest" with no time off for good behavior.

So, I'm going to be the bitch who tells it like it is. When I can't live alone, go to Zumba class, and enjoy stimulating conversations with smart people who may or may not be my age, I'll be looking for a final exit.

Who knows? This option might force nursing homes to get better.

As a marketing pro, I'd argue that giving out cyanide pills could end up making the elderly life worth living. If we could choose to die before we got to the nursing home, the homes would soon be empty. The "care managers" would be motivated to find a way to fill them up again.

Imagine the ad: "No need to take your cyanide pill! Come to Magnificent Manor."

Of course, some of us would take the pill anyway. But I bet a lot of things would get a lot better.

Chapter 7: "I'm a smartass, not a sage."

"It is easy to attribute wisdom to the old because wisdom can mean anything to anyone." Susan Jacoby, *Never Say Die*, p 187-188.

Here's yet another place where the stereotypes trip over each other.

On the one hand, you're supposed to be a wise old sage.

On the other hand, many people simply assume that your mental faculties will decline as you pass fifty. You're far too incompetent to hold down a paying job, they say, unless you're a celebrity or a Senator or, God help us, a President.

Does everybody get wiser with age?

A sixty-plus person might deny climate change, insist that abstinence is the cure for teen sex, and believe fervently that anyone who doesn't share her beliefs will go straight to hell — literally.

Another sixty-plus person might write technical letters to her Senator, citing research reports to support her view on climate change. She might advocate for a Madam Millie brothel to initiate young men into sex and believe "hell" is a meaningless swear word.

Who hasn't encountered women whose mothers promulgated awful advice about child-rearing based on their own background? It's usually a cohort effect -- someone who grew up in the early fifties who still believes, "That kid just needs a good swat."

Blame The Intern: A New Image for Older Executives

It was the last day of my vacation in Seattle. I suggested to my friend George, "We should go see a movie. Something light and fun." Since I have a career blog and study issues of ageism, *The Intern* with Robert DeNiro seemed a perfect choice.

The Intern is light and does have some fun moments. But mostly the movie recycles one stereotype after another.

The writers need a premise to get Robert DeNiro into a start-up tech company as an intern. So instead of having him apply for a position based on skills, they come up with a bizarre premise. The Robert DeNiro character gets assigned to the Anne Hathaway character for the unlikely purpose of softening her edges.

When Robert DeNiro read his application letter aloud, I whispered to George (I rarely talk in a movie, but this was a horror show), "This guy needs a career coach." His letter was all about him: he was lonely and isolated and wanted to work. His forty-plus years of business experience? Irrelevant to him ... and sadly, to the company as well.

The stereotypes continue when Robert DeNiro wears a suit and carries a briefcase, reinforcing the notion that seniors prefer traditional formality and refuse to adapt to corporate culture.

Give me a break. Today's sixty-somethings grew up wearing blue jeans, shorts, and business casual. I wear sneakers to networking events and nobody bats an eye.

Of course, the DeNiro character doesn't know how to use Facebook. He wouldn't be an "older person" in a movie if he did.

I know 70-year-olds who are not only active on social media but also are setting up WordPress blogs and editing movies. And I know thirty-year-olds who can barely handle their emails, let alone set up blogs or Instagram accounts.

We don't have to rely on anecdotal evidence. An HBR article reports research showing that innovators are more likely to be over 50 than under 30; the young kids in the garage are likely to be the exception, not the rule.

In *The Intern*, the Robert DeNiro character does know how to make himself useful in a new corporate setting, even if he's ignored. He's got business savvy, although the analyses he performs seem pretty simplistic and the Hathaway character should be getting reports generated automatically. His people skills are so strong he reinforces another stereotype: the over-sixty set now has to be wise and kind as well as humble, heroic, and good with children.

DeNiro even hops into an unfamiliar car and drives easily all over New York City, something most people can't do whether they're nineteen or ninety.

Meanwhile, the Hathaway character turns into a helpless, whiny stereotypical old-style female. Her life is out of control. She shares personal information inappropriately. But she's got the main qualification to be taken seriously and run a company (alas, not only in the movies). She's young and attractive.

The movie ends with the worst stereotype of aging.

Robert DeNiro begins his internship eager to work. Like many people, he derived his life's purpose from meaningful paid work, not volunteering or "leaving a legacy." In our society, you don't get taken seriously till you get paid for what you do.

Unlike young entry-level interns, DeNiro won't be rewarded with a paid position in this company or anywhere else. Older adults - and "older" starts at forty-something in most companies - just aren't wanted. Employers might complain about their need for technology skills, but they find reasons not to hire "mature" graduates of boot camp tech courses.

Sure enough, at the movie's end, we see DeNiro heading back to retirement, relieved to re-join his morning tai chi class.

If he were a real person? Give him about 2 weeks and he'll be wishing his internship had turned out to be a real job.

Only if you're old...

Imagine a movie with a gay hero who swishes onto the basketball court wearing makeup and discovering he can indeed make three-point shots ... although he was brought onto the team as a gesture to diversity and a way to get livelier press coverage.

Imagine a movie with an African-American heroine who's hired as an office temp, then uses her house cleaning skills (honed by years as a maid) to make the boss look good, serves watermelon on coffee break, introduces an office hip-hop competition ("got rhythm?") and insists on wearing African dress to work.

Ludicrous? Yes. Offensive? Absolutely. But so are movies about older people who can't use computers and hang on to a 90s wardrobe.

Contribute your knowledge without becoming an intern, sage, or special snowflake.

The intern trope has resonated with other authors and, apparently, with company CEOs who brighten up at the thought of cheap labor. In all these narratives the senior male was the condescending sage and change agent, hired solely because of his previous career status.

The premise is that "older" people can join companies as "interns." They learn technology and social media strategy while contributing their business "wisdom."

The truth is, there's nothing new about the "older intern" role except the focus on age and unflattering job title.

Corporate America has always welcomed senior executives of all ages who had something special to contribute. They might have to learn a new industry or acquire new skills, but they're paid market rates from the very first day.

Chris Conley's best-selling book, *Wisdom at Work,* recasts the "respected senior executive" as a humble newcomer. After years of running his own business, Conley got an invitation from Airbnb: Come use your skills to help us.

Conley defines himself and his relationship with Airbnb entirely in terms of age. He even asks a fellow employee, "Aren't you old for an engiener?"

He wonders how he'll feel about getting a performance review from someone who's twenty years younger.

Is he serious? Surely, he knows his performance reviews will be pro forma, if they occur at all; he's not just another name on the payroll.

It's not at all unusual for someone entering a new job, at any age, to experience a steep learning curve. Smart companies happily subsidize this learning curve, knowing they'll reap the benefits when the new employee gets up to speed.

When my under-40 friend Diane moved from banking to a tech startup, she brought her knowledge of Agile software and project management; she had to learn a new faster-paced, more laid-back culture, as well as a new industry. After a couple of years, she moved again to a retail chain, as a more senior project manager. She had to learn new software, new management styles, and yet another industry.

Nobody asked her to be an intern.

The Social Responsibilities of A Sage

"My husband gave advice to a guy who's feeling discouraged with dating," someone posted to a Facebook group.

"I overheard him advising the guy, 'You can practice by talking to women in their 70s, just to learn how to relate to women as real people, and maybe get some advice on how to approach younger women.'"

So now the role of an "older woman" is to be an unpaid relationship coach to a clueless guy.

Of course, she's the expert on how to deal with women in their twenties, since it's been a while and dating norms have, um, changed just a little in the last fifty years.

Of course, she's a wise old crone. Never mind that she might have had a string of affairs throughout her life, most of which ended badly, mostly involving guys with drinking problems who left her broke.

Or maybe she's always been an uptight prude who believed women should "save it for marriage." That'll be helpful.

Or she's wary of casual dating because she remembers the vulnerability she experienced herself, growing up in the days before birth control pills were widely available.

Or she's a gay woman who's hardly the expert to advise men of a certain age.

Nope, none of this matters. She's in her 70s. That makes her wise.

A truckload of books supports the notion of wise old people. There's even a whole book called *From Age-ing to Sage-ing: A Revolutionary Approach to Growing Older*.

The author sees older people as contributing wisdom (gratuitously, of course, without pay) Somehow the grandparents are supposed to impart their experience to younger generations of families. The word "busybody" seems more fitting than "family counselor."

But a sage isn't supposed to be knowledgeable in an ordinary, useful way. Sages offer big-picture wisdom with limited value.

In his book *Happiness Is A Choice You Make*, Leland (p 33) quotes Monika Ardelt, an academic who researches the elderly: "Older people still have a lot to offer us, even if only how to die and age gracefully."

Still have? Where did that come from? And this quote really isn't about age: it's about anyone, of any age, who's facing death in the short term.

At Hubert Humphrey's funeral, Senator Walter Mondale eulogized, "he taught us how to live, and finally, he taught us how to die." Humphrey was just sixty-six years old.

The problem is that for most of the time we're alive and old, we're nowhere near dying. Neither is anyone around us. So this wisdom is so highly specialized it's not needed in the world of commerce and society.

Who wants to hire a sage -- someone who will pontificate theoretically while younger folks get the job done? Someone who can teach us how to die but has trouble mastering the most commonly used software? This image doesn't do a thing to help older people get integrated into the workforce.

Leave the sage on the spice rack in the kitchen.

When I think of "sage" I tend to think of the spice you use on poultry. Sageing your home can also be a way to expel the bad spirits. If that's the kind of sageing you've got in mind, I'm all for it.

And speaking of spirits, I'm not crazy about comparing "older people" to wines that grow better as they age. Remember: these wines must be stored in a dark, dry basement so they won't go sour.

Chapter 8: "Being old isn't sexy... but I'll settle for being a sexy old broad."

"Seventy-nine-year-old Jane Fonda is doing for vibrators what forty-four-year-old Jane Fonda did for aerobics videos..." — Chicago Tribune.

"[Our] culture doesn't like people with wrinkles to be talking about sex... But the fastest-growing demographic in the world is older women, and a lot of them are doing it very pleasurably." - Jane Fonda, quoted in an interview with W.

An aging broad calls the police.

"When I look in the mirror," she says, "I see this strange old woman who's gotten into my house. She follows me around. She stands in front of me so I don't see myself as I really am."

The police come. Nobody's there. As you've undoubtedly guessed, she doesn't recognize herself.

Swear off talking about appearance and practice swearing in general.

So much attention gets paid to changes in appearance as "we" get older. That's usually how it's written, too.

You'll find tons of articles on how to wear make-up "after fifty." I read them. But since my eye doctor warned me about some weird condition I picked up — not age-related but gets aggravated by makeup— I've had to withdraw from those discussions.

I admit to being a bit of a hypocrite. When the same eye doctor said a lid lift would do wonders for my vision, as well as my appearance, I jumped at it. I'd lost a lot of peripheral vision, so it was a legitimate medical expense. The insurance company paid.

Otherwise, I wear sunglasses and a hat. Anyway, when you swear a lot, people tend to look away.

"I'm not my face or my hair."

You're supposed to dye your hair … or you're supposed to go natural, depending on which magazine you read.

Frankly, this discussion seems really, really dumb. Going grey isn't about accepting your age. It's about how you want to look, whether you're twenty-five or seventy-five.

Some people have gorgeous silver hair. My friend Sally has a beautiful black and white pattern, like chocolate syrup swirls on vanilla ice cream. She shouldn't hit the dye pot.

Some aging broads have magnificent white hair. Who could forget the late Barbara Bush?

They're not going grey. They're going gorgeous.

Me? I've been coloring my hair since I was twenty-five, but I'm pretty sure it's an ugly shade of washed-out gray. Besides, my hair is curly, which makes me look older even with colored hair. During a humid summer, the frizz costs all my credibility. Straight hair definitely gives you an edge. Unless an allergy develops, I'll keep my colorist busy till I'm dead.

I don't mind wrinkles at all. I just get frustrated when they make it easier to stereotype. It's like wearing a Halloween witch mask.

Many comedians like to tell jokes about growing old and getting chin hair.

Chin hair? Like that's our biggest problem?

I bought some hair removal creams. They mostly don't work. I'm far too squeamish for waxing. I won't even get my ears pierced.

So mostly I don't think much about it. In my darker moments, I figure people are saying things like, "What's wrong with her? Doesn't she know…" But then I get distracted and the mood passes.

Anyway, I don't feel like I'm my face. I'm more like my butt.

An orthopedic surgeon told me, "When you work your glutes, you're less likely to have hip fractures."

But more importantly, I wear leggings and shorts, and who wants to jiggle around where everyone can see you? I literally work my ass off in the gym for buns of steel.

My butt says "thirties." My face says, "Don't get too close."

Being Invisible: The Role Assigned To "Older Women"

In a *New York Times* article, "The Gift of Menopause," Margaret Renkl writes, "I was never a woman who turned heads, but menopause has made me invisible, and I love being invisible. I don't know if it's menopause or simply aging, but time's winged chariot has freed me from bikinis, among other things."

It's all part of the "growing older" package, she says,

"which also includes... the ability to say no (which gives you the gift of time).

"What a relief to be rid of trying to please others, to conform to society's idea of beauty. I don't want to be sexy at seventy, though good for Goldie Hawn and Diane Keaton and Diane Sawyer, Helen Mirren, and all the others who seem to pull it off."

As often happens with *The New York Times*, the comments were more insightful than the article:

"Actually, I'm tired of women "embracing" their invisibility when they don't have a choice. I do want to be noticed, taken seriously in a conversation whether work-related or social."

"I'm a 69-year-old woman, but I'm six feet tall. Believe me, I never feel invisible."

And best of all:

"I hope you understand that you do not speak for me, or for all women. Some of us don't fit the mold, and we never will. And we're glad we don't. And we're not invisible. We're confident. We know we matter."

Who cares about looking "fuckable?" Not us.

Sigrid Nunez's novel, *What Are You Going Through*, includes a scene of a female professor introducing a well-known guest speaker. Nunez categorizes the professor as ...

"Someone at pains for it to be known that, although smart and well educated, although a feminist and a woman in a position of power, the lady is no frump, no boring nerd, no sexless harridan. And so what if she's past a certain age. The cling of the skirt, the height of the heels, the scarlet mouth and tinted hair . . . everything says: I'm still fuckable."

If you think about it, the term "fuckable" is extremely demeaning. It says, "I'm attractive to men who are looking for a sex object."

93

A certified Bitchy Broad doesn't care if people think she's still fuckable. She'd rather say, "Fuck you!" to those judgmental people (and maybe give them the finger while she's at it).

There's a reason a lot of us watch the movie *Harold and Maude* for the twentieth time. Do we have crushes on inappropriately younger men? Sure, although none of us will admit it on the record.

Nor will a Bitchy Broad relate to this gloomy comment by Arthur Krystal in *The New Yorker* magazine, Why We Can't Tell the Truth About Aging:

"It's not just energy or sexual prowess but the thrill of anticipation… the rush of excitement…the first moment when clothes drop to the floor? Who the hell wants to tear his or her clothes off at seventy-five?"

There's a guy who hasn't watched *Harold and Maude* even once.

The New Me-Too Moments: Unwanted Touching

I pretty much escaped the "me too" moments, probably because I was a lethal combination of outspoken and naive. I had a reputation for not keeping my mouth shut. If someone assaulted me, I wouldn't go hide in shame. I'd tell the world.

And I lived in a bubble: I probably got invited to do all sorts of things when I thought they were just inviting me to join them over a double cheese pizza.

But now it's 2019. I'm on a bus, ready to exit at my stop, when I feel a vise-like grip on my right arm. A righteous-looking female stranger stands there, firmly, like a US Marshal making sure her prisoner gets to court on time. She's worried that I'll fall as the bus lurches down the block.

A law enforcement officer once told me, "Never touch a cop by surprise. She'll come out swinging."

I consider pretending I'm in law enforcement and taking a swing of my own. But I need to get where I'm going and causing a scene on the Number 17 bus can be dicey. Half the people are on their cell phones talking to their methadone clinics. The other half are off-duty cops talking to their confidential informants about the people who are talking to their methadone clinics.

And I never learned how to knock someone flat.

Instead, I just shake her off with a firm, "I'm fine, thanks," and look to see if she's left a bruise.

Another time, a man sitting next to me touches my back as I get up to leave the bus, no doubt assuming I'm too frail to navigate the short distance to the door. I'm actually on the way to the gym. This time I say, "Please don't touch me." He's offended. Who cares?

Or I'm in West Philadelphia, en route to a book discussion event for Penn alums. Walking out of a store, I'm adjusting my backpack when I feel creepy little hands fumbling around back there. Am I being robbed?

A tiny white-haired woman has decided, on her own, to help me straighten my backpack. I try to be charitable and assume she's bored out of her mind and desperate to relate to another human. But if there were a legal way to flatten her, I'd do it.

Then there was the moment I exited the #40 bus at 3rd and Pine, carrying my gym bag and two heavy Whole Foods bags. As I stepped down a serious-looking fortyish man with glasses reached out from behind me and grabbed my upper arm.

Me: "What are you doing?"

Man: "I'm helping you down the steps."

Me: "If you really want to help, why don't you just take one of these bags?"

Man: "They're too heavy."

The funny part is, I'm probably in better shape than any of these helper wannabes.

Alas, the parts that are strong and solid are covered up by my winter parka. Anyway, it's probably not a good idea to respond with something like, "My butt is firmer than yours." Might give them ideas about where else I need help.

ME-ME MOMENTS

One day I walk into the ceramics studio where I take classes, during open-work hours. A bunch of fifty-plus women are putting the finishing touches on their sculptures. They aren't talking about knitting or grandchildren or their last visit to the doctor. They are talking about sex toys... specifically, vibrators.

One woman seeks advice about which one to buy. She's going through some significant cash flow issues and doesn't have a lot of spare change. But a vibrator is high on her priority list.

No surprise. The internet is filled with lists of "10 Best Vibrators for Women Over 50."

After all, a lot of women don't want to start a relationship that will end with them taking care of some old guy with prostate problems. Not when we've invested twenty months with them, not twenty years. Fortunately, we have other options.

You'll rarely hear the word "masturbation" in connection with sex toys. That's an ugly word. Let's call it "self-pleasuring."

In the Netflix comedy Grace and Frankie, Jane Fonda's character planned a vibrator designed for older women with large print on the directions and light near the on-off switch.

Dr. Christiane Northrup's book, *Goddesses Never Age*, goes into great detail on self-pleasuring. She doesn't recommend vibrators but acknowledges that many women will want to use them.

She's unusual. Most doctors are clueless. The fastest way to make a doctor blush is to bring up the topic of vibrators. I saw this firsthand when I had my micro-surgery for an ovarian cyst back in 2009.

Doc: "Now for two weeks don't put anything into your vagina. No tampons. No penises.

Me: "Vibrators?"

Doc: "Um…" (big blush)

They should listen to Dr. Lauren Streicher, medical director of Northwestern Memorial Hospital's Center for Sexual Medicine and Menopause.

Quoted in a *Chicago Tribune* article, Dr. Streicher says, "When I teach medical students, I tell them: Don't ever say to a woman, 'Do you have a vibrator?' That is the wrong question. What you say is, 'When you use your vibrator …'"

It's about time.

Never mind how we look on the outside. Inside, many of us feel like Samantha in *Sex and the City*.

The truth is, by the time you qualify for Aging Bad-Ass Broad status, you've probably been around the block a few times.

Maybe you've got a romantic interest who's age-appropriate: a spouse who's been around a long time, a special friend you met online, or someone who's in your social circle.

Maybe you've come alive to a new sexuality: you might decide you like women or you're ready for a different type of guy.

Or maybe you've learned to love your own company.

Getting a lover would be nice, but after a certain point I'm not ready to say, "for better or worse," because a good part of the future will undoubtedly be "worse."

Definitely not ready to say, "in sickness and in health." If I'd been married for twenty years, I'd be happy to play nurse to an 80-something with prostate problems.

Now? I've lost my nurturing vibe, or more likely they left off the nurturing gene when I was born.

Besides, if you bed someone, you'll be going to doctors for checkups and infections. The doc will be rude and patronizing. You'll sit in her waiting room for an hour and then she'll try to sell you on a bunch of tests you don't need. You'd better really love that guy.

There's a reason DIY sounds good to a lot of women.

Forget "Grandma got run over by a reindeer."

Grandma just got herself a merry little Christmas from the local sex toy shop.

Chapter 9:
"I'm not depressed. I'm mad as hell."

"Contrary to what many people think, depression is not a normal part of growing older." - Jane Brody in *The New York Times*.

Here's yet another place the stereotypes collide with each other.

Stereotype #1: People naturally get happier as they get older. They're more patient with screw-ups, especially in medical settings. They don't complain.

Stereotype #2: People naturally get more depressed as they get older. This assumption seems behind the many articles on "Depression in Seniors."

Let's look more closely at each story.

Stereotype #1: "Older people are happier than younger adults.

Time magazine reported a study of over 1500 people from 20 to 99 in San Diego. The study was cross-sectional, which meant the responses were simply grouped by age.

Hopefully, you immediately recognize a cohort effect. At one time, people - especially women - were brought up to be polite. Admitting you're angry or dissatisfied would seem ill-mannered and inappropriate. More contemporary women won't share these inhibitions.

The New York Times ran an article, "Want to Be Happy? Think Like an Old Person." The article's author, John Leland (the same author who recognized the danger of calling people "dear"), interviewed people in their eighties and nineties, living on their own or in a high-quality nursing home, with relatives available to visit them.

"When the elders described their lives," the article says, "they focused not on their declining abilities but on things that they could still do and that they found rewarding. As [one interviewee] said, 'I try not to think about bad things. It's not good for old people to complain."

Why are they so happy?

Once again, we're getting cohort effects. People in this group were brought up to share beliefs about "old people" and about complaining. Like children, we're supposed to be seen and not heard.

As a free adult, you recognize when your life isn't working and you take proactive steps to change it. To change your life, you need to complain about bad service, refuse unwanted medical treatment, demand appropriate medical treatment, write to legislators and government officials, write letters to the editor, comment on newspaper articles, and even stand up to authority figures.

Doing any of those things as an "older" person (especially if you're female) will get you marked as a complainer or even as a bitch. I'd own that identity with pride.

Now contrast that with …

Stereotype #2: Depression has been frequently associated with aging.

An article on WebMD notes that depression among older adults is "common" but not "normal."

I am not a clinician or expert on depression. My goal is to question the tendency to assume older people are clinically depressed, especially if they realistically don't have a lot to live for.

The CDC's official website argues that depression is not a "normal part of aging" and should be treated. However, the website notes, "Depression is more common in people who also have other illnesses (such as heart disease or cancer) or whose function becomes limited."

An article on the website of the American Psychological Association suggests similarly, "The feelings of hopelessness and isolation that often spur thoughts of suicide are more prevalent among older adults, especially those with disabilities or confined to nursing homes."

A desire to escape an unbearable life should not be confused with depression. It's worth repeating: Patrick Henry wasn't depressed when he said, "Give me liberty or give me death."

The article's recommendations build on stereotypes: "Because elderly people tend to be less amenable to lifestyle changes, they may be reluctant to adopt new habits or do things that their peers find highly enjoyable."

In other words, if you don't conform to the norm of what "most people your age" enjoy, you're depressed.

When a teenager prefers classical music to the current popular band, do we say she's depressed? Do we say, "Come on, kids your age love this music!" Or do we encourage her to find others who share her musical tastes, regardless of age?

Conflicting Views About Depression

Millions of people of all ages get diagnosed as "depressed." You probably know at least one or two people who are taking anti-depressants. Some people get caught up in biologically based depression that doesn't go away.

But one thing seems clear. Experts don't agree on the diagnosis and treatment of depression.

Writing in the *Huffington Post*, Dr. Mark Hyman says, "'Depression' is simply a label" that we give to people with a variety of symptoms, including "depressed mood," sleeplessness, hopelessness, indecisiveness or no longer finding pleasure in certain life activities.

But, he goes on to say, this definition says nothing about the causes of depression. He argues for an anti-inflammatory diet and a series of potential dietary deficiencies.

Too quick to attach a "Depressed Person" label to an older person

Studies consistently report that depressed people -- as many as half of those with depression -- have not gotten help. Just google "percent of people with depression who are untreated." It's hard to get good numbers, because, by definition, those who have not been treated have most likely not been diagnosed by a clinician.

But it's also true that many people are falsely diagnosed with depression. Writing in *The Atlantic Monthly*, Lindsay Abrams argues that as many as 60% of people diagnosed with depression do not meet the clinical criteria for depression. She refers to the diagnostic criteria of the DSM -- Diagnostic and Statistical Manual used by the vast majority of clinicians.

The DSM itself has come under criticism, notably in Paula Caplan's book, *They Think We're Crazy*.

And psychiatric diagnosis is particularly tricky, says Steven Hatch, in his book *Snowball in A Blizzard*. The diagnosis often says more about the psychiatrist than the "patient."

Hatch points to the Rosenhan effect. In a study that would likely be forbidden today, ordinary "normal" people checked themselves into mental institutions, claiming to hear voices. Other than the initial statement, they told the truth. Psychiatrists interpreted all their actions as symptoms of mental illness. Ironically, the "real" patients caught on. They thought these pseudo-patients were doctors working undercover.

Older people get stereotypes on steroids.

We get the stereotype, "Older people suffer more from depression." Now a lot of older people get falsely diagnosed.

Then we get the stereotype, "Depressed people aren't rational." And now there's a pseudo-scientific rationale to ignore the reasonable wishes and actions of older people...which leads to extreme frustration and feelings that support the "depressed" diagnosis.

Add another common belief reported by WebMD: "The stigma attached to mental illness and psychiatric treatment is even more powerful among older people."

That's a cohort effect for sure.

Maybe people born before the 1950s associate psychotherapy with stigma. Today? For many people of a certain generation and background, it's no big deal.

"Of course I have a therapist. Doesn't everybody?"

The only raised eyebrows come when someone wonders, "Does insurance really cover ten years of therapy?"

Moreover, getting a diagnosis of "depressed" or "anxious" can add a layer of complexity to your medical care, especially when you get older. It's already difficult to be taken seriously when you report a medical problem. I doubt there's a female over 40 who hasn't heard at least once, "It's probably all in your mind."

Add an anxiety diagnosis to your medical record and you're in for some drama with your next office visit.

Writing for *The New York Times*, Jane Brody claims, "Primary care practitioners are also crucial to suicide prevention among the elderly because older people, and especially older men, are unlikely to seek out and accept mental health services but *are often seen by family doctors and nurses within days or weeks of a suicide.*" [emphasis added]

Think about that one. It's all too easy to feel depressed after an encounter with a "primary care practitioner..." not to mention their techs, nurses, surgical coordinators, and waiting rooms.

A more helpful approach to understanding depression: Look at the context.

Johann Hari introduces a new story. He's a journalist and science reporter, and his findings have generated some controversy. However, as a non-doctor and official medical skeptic, I find his perspective provides a useful framework to discuss depression and aging.

Scientists around the world have begun to question what "everyone knows:" the belief that depression is caused by brain chemistry, so chemicals can help people feel better. Most of these studies were conducted by drug companies. When the scientists got access to raw data - including studies never reported to the FDA -- they found that anti-depressants helped only a very small number of depressed people.

What most clinicians don't do, Hari argues, is ask about context. When did you first begin feeling depressed? What was going on in your world and your life? Did you just experience a painful loss?

Hari suggests that depression comes from a loss of connection. We get depressed when we're disconnected from people, from nature, from meaningful values, from respect, and -- most critically for older people -- a secure and meaningful future.

Hari doesn't discuss age effects. But I can't help noting that older people get disconnected from all those things. They're often not taken seriously, especially if they're women.

Older people are -- by simple math -- often disconnected from what Hari calls a "secure and meaningful future." Therefore, they're more vulnerable to what's commonly called "depression."

3 reasons why older people get disconnected

(1) Uncertainty:

As you get older, you are increasingly unable to make confident predictions about where and how you'll be in ten years. The gap gets even wider as you age.

Here's one way a person might experience uncertainty over the years:

Age 45: By 55 you'll still be able to do everything you can do now, barring an unexpected illness or accident. Your major barrier to work will be age discrimination, not your own abilities.

Age 55: Age 65 seems far away. Your life will look different a year from now, if only because you become eligible for Medicare and (shortly afterward) Social Security, if you're in the United States.

Age 65: If you're healthy now, you'll probably be able to continue on the same path ten years from now. You might hit a speed bump as you approach and pass 70. Most people are healthier than they expect -- certainly far healthier than the stereotype -- but the probabilities have shifted.

Age 75: You're likely to experience physical changes in the next 10 years. This change isn't inevitable: think of Olga Kotelko, running marathons in her nineties. But when you play the probabilities, you're not likely to be an Olga. Who wouldn't be at least a little bummed?

Age 85: "Ten years from now? You must be kidding…" You might be fully functional, driving and traveling. Or you might be locked away in a care home with no quality of life.

Age 90: "Where's that one-way business class ticket to Switzerland? I'm keeping it in a safe place."

(2) Loss of physical functions, which in turn means loss of liberty.

As Susan Jacoby notes in *Never Say Die*, it's common for medical professionals to assume older people are "depressed" when they're in chronic pain that can't be relieved by medication with no hope of getting better...or when they find their conditions of life intolerable due to restrictions on their lifestyle.

Some people believe that anyone who wants to die must be depressed. Others -- and I'm in this camp -- believe that we need to distinguish a desire to avoid helplessness and pain from depression that has been associated with suicide.

Nobody said Patrick Henry was clinically depressed when he said, "Give me liberty or give me death." Nobody administered a Rorschach to a World War II spy pilot parachuting his way into enemy territory, quickly swallowing his cyanide pill.

Not much different if you're headed for one of those nursing homes.

(3) Loss of earning power.

Of course, money isn't everything. But as I say in the next chapter, being a Rich Bitch is better.

Depression seems to be a completely appropriate response to age discrimination.

When you're denied opportunities to earn money, you're denied access to many joyful experiences. If you're expected to socialize in a limited circle, you lose out on meaningful conversations and connections.

Experiencing daily insults, not being taken seriously, getting treated like a child ... who wouldn't be depressed?

The only alternative is to speak out and speak up. Anger can lead to change. In fact, when you look at civil rights movements, you'll find change happens when people get mad enough to say, "We're not putting up with this anymore."

Anger doesn't have to be violent. It can take the form of letters to legislators, reports to your Attorney General, and polite but strong responses to everyday insults.

Of course, you're not expected to respond this way. They'll be thinking "bitch" even if they don't say it aloud.

Once, in airport security, a cocky young TSA agent kept calling me "Mom." Without thinking, I said, "That is very rude. 'Ma'am' is polite. 'Mom' is an insult."

Later I thought, "That was pretty dumb. You don't want to mess with the TSA." But my reaction was automatic, and I suspect he knew he was being rude. He just figured I was a nice little lady who wouldn't speak up.

Next time he'll know better.

Chapter 10: "Nothing wrong with being a rich bitch. Pay me what I'm worth."

"You can be young without money, but you can't be old without it. You've got to be old with money because to be old without it is just too awful, you've got to be one or the other, either young or with money, you can't be old and without it. That's the truth, Brick..."

—Tennessee Williams, Cat on a Hot Tin Roof

"They say money is not the key to happiness. Give me enough money and I'll buy a key." - Joan Rivers

A lady in a brand-new Volvo is poised to back into a parking spot when a young guy driving a sports car steals the spot out from under her.

"Why'd you do that?" she demands angrily.

"Because I'm young and quick," comes his snotty reply.

As he walks away, hears loud banging noises. Sure enough, the lady repeatedly hits his car with her Volvo. Now he's driving a wreck.

"Why'd you do that?" he demands.

"Because I'm old and rich," she says.

This old chestnut is all over the Internet. In real life, the lady could be arrested for intentionally damaging someone's property. With a good lawyer and an offer to buy the man a new car, she'd probably get off lightly.

The story makes a point every aging broad should remember. Money allows you to reject the Miss Congeniality role and embrace your role as a Rich Bitch.

Stop telling us, "Money isn't everything."

Of course, money isn't everything. Friends, family, and dogs are more important than money. But the truth is, the more money you have, the more choices you can make about how you spend time with friends and family. You'll be able to keep your dogs -- and yourself -- healthier and happier.

And the more money you have, the more ways you can enjoy yourself as you grow older.

You might decide you want to serve hot dogs at your 80th birthday party … but you have the option to serve a catered meal or a gourmet sit-down dinner.

You can say "no thanks" to Medicare reimbursement plans and hire your own specialists. You can choose concierge medicine, where doctors keep their appointments on time, and you get treated like a person instead of a number with a diagnosis.

You can go overseas for a very special vacation, for the medical care you need, or for access to assisted dying. You can get a good haircut and feel pampered in a high-end salon. You can hire a personal trainer when your insurance-paid physical therapist sets up double-booked appointments where you spend an hour to get twenty minutes of attention from a visibly bored provider.

You can donate to your favorite charities and save a hundred stray cats. You can live in a place that allows dogs – and spoil your dog rotten.

But even more important, you'll get treated differently. Walk into a room confidently, claim your bitchy birthright, and you'll command respect. Sure, you can do this without money, but it's tougher.

You need money but the stereotypes are killing your opportunities to earn it.

A few years ago, career advisor Liz Ryan wrote a column for *Forbes*, unabashedly titled, "The Ugly Truth About Age Discrimination. A job seeker reported the interviewer who told him, point-blank, he was a little "long in the tooth" for the job.

"Isn't this age discrimination?"

Sure, but there's not much you can do. If the company hires a well-qualified person of any age, you'll have trouble making a case.

Ryan goes on to say, "I hear more examples of age discrimination than I hear about sex discrimination, racial discrimination, and every other kind put together." If you're past a certain age, you won't be a bit surprised.

She advises job hunters of all ages to focus on the hiring manager's pain. Get out of the police lineup. Stop giving "sheeplike" answers that encourage companies to compare you to the younger applicants.

That's not a bad strategy. Maybe it even works, sometimes. But my advice is a little different. I tell everyone to prepare for self-employment, starting at age 45.

It's not a career: it's a merry-go-round.

Once I asked an editor at a publishing conference, "What books do you need for your line?"

He replied, "I'd love to get a book on How to Get a Good Job After 60."

Pause.

"And it would be even better if you could add, 'Easily.'"

Yeah, right.

In a Dummies book, *Getting The Job You Want After 50*, the author identifies "ten great jobs for workers over 50." She says she chose them because of growing demand, which should translate to opportunities; and "you're probably qualified right now to do any of them, although you may need to get a certification to prove it."

If that isn't chirpy-talk, I don't know what is. For some of these jobs you need a lot more than an easy-to-get certification. The ten jobs include financial advisor, fitness instructor, massage therapist, and patient care advocate.

I gave the book a one-star rating and wrote a particularly scathing review. One of my friends ghosted me shortly afterward.

Embarking on a career is like getting on the merry-go-round.

Sooner or later, it's going to stop. When you're young, you'll be able to get off and move to another merry-go-round. Or you'll have the luxury of waiting till it starts up again.

When you're defined as "old," you're already on the merry-go-round. You're fine if you keep going. You can stay forever, till you fall off your horse.

But when the merry-go-round stops, you're stuck. The other merry-go-rounds won't take you. If you wait till you start up again, you could find yourself pushed off your horse and replaced.

Competence won't keep you on the merry-go-round.

Elizabeth White's book, *55, Underemployed and Faking Normal*, focuses on professionals and managers who have fallen off the merry-go-round.

Ms. White gives voice to many of our nightmares. In her fifties, she was solidly in the zone of "old enough for age discrimination, too young for social security." With degrees from Johns Hopkins and Harvard, she lost her consulting contracts during the 2008 recession and never rebounded.

Finally, she posted an article, "You Know Me" on a popular online blog. She wrote about being hidden behind nice clothes. Finding a way to avoid splitting the check in a restaurant because she couldn't afford to pay for the drinks and desserts her friends ordered. Buying the $1.99 size box of detergent.

Ms. White's premise is, "You have to learn to live with less. Sometimes a lot less." She writes about taking Greyhound buses to business meetings, giving up cable and gym memberships, and hitting up friends and family for loans during the toughest times.

When you reach a certain age, she says, getting arrested might be easier than getting a job interview.

Forget about looking to the government for solutions.

"Age is treated as a second-class civil right," said Dan Kohrman, attorney for AARP, as quoted in Gail Collins's book, *No Stopping*

Us Now. Age discrimination cases, particularly among women, are particularly difficult to litigate.

Collins explains bitterly and brilliantly:

"Some employers – particularly in office situations—prefer female underlings who are young and attractive…Thanks to previous Supreme Court decisions, if they're charged with age bias, [employers] can point to their good record with older men. And if gender comes up, they can point to their large supply of younger women."

Option 1: Choose a merry-go-round that won't stop and jump on early.

Lots of jobs will allow you to stay once you're established -- you just can't break in after you're 35 or so. You need to be safely inside by the time you hit the magic 50, if not earlier.

A few years ago, I was on the phone with an airline reservations agent. As I tried to play the age card ("I'm old … I need to change this flight") she responded right back, "I'm 72."

Wow. You can be an airline reservations agent when you're 72.

The catch? She'd been working for the airline for over 20 years. There's no way she'd get hired at 72 or probably even 62. But once she was there, she got to stay.

When I lived in Seattle, I kept hearing about a bus driver who was going strong at 80. All the drivers knew about him. Apparently, if you can pass the physical you can keep driving forever.

He was extremely wealthy, they told me. He just drove the bus for something to do. He preferred the late-night route covering the upscale Queen Anne Hill.

My friend Deborah chose law as her merry-go-round. Deborah is a lawyer who prefers to work as a paralegal. In her 40s she moved to Seattle, where she found work with a law firm in her specialty of medical malpractice. She was a superstar! The firm invited her to take the bar exam and work with them as an attorney.

At age 50 she studied for the Washington State Bar and passed the first time. She was then recruited to work in a hospital in risk management, recruited back to the law firm as a paralegal (at her request) and then ... yes, back to a hospital as a manager again. She built on years of experience to gain employment.

Today Deborah lives in her dream city in Southern California. Close to sixty, she works remotely as a paralegal. She's earned and saved enough to enjoy life on her own terms.

Option 2: Jump off the merry-go-round when and where you choose.

You can't prevent all disasters. You can become economically challenged through no fault of your own. A single illness can decimate your savings, especially if you live in the United States.

But while you're still on a payroll, you can take steps to plan your post-corporate career.

Elizabeth White recommends creating Resilience Circles as support groups so you'll feel less alone. The truth is, "We're all in this together" will only take you so far.

While you're still on a payroll, see if you can afford to hire a career consultant or life coach.

If they're any good at all, they won't encourage you to smile and sign up for food stamps. They'll help you move to a new career, which might involve braving the path to entrepreneurship.

One of Elizabeth White's interviewees acknowledged getting help from a life coach who offered him some free assistance. Imagine what he'd get if he could pay for half a dozen full sessions.

Option 3: Build your own merry-go-round with a side hustle.

For the vast majority of people who want to age with pride and independence, there's only one solution.

Give yourself the gift of a side hustle. If you've never worked on your own, you'll need to start early: entrepreneurship is a state of mind. You can start at any time. But as with most things, time is not kind to those who wait.

Pick a side hustle where you're not dependent on one employer. Whether you moonlight for Uber or do the books for a medium-sized company, you're one decision away from unemployment.

Don't worry about prestige.

I've known people who said, "I can't be a cat sitter. What will the neighbors think?"

You're not a cat sitter. You're a business owner. The neighbors will admire your drive and motivation. Rich people admire entrepreneurs. You might even become rich yourself. Some dog walkers earn more than their clients.

When I'm writing copy, I want to earn the market rate for copywriters at my level of skill and experience. I don't need to be paid as a business executive or business professor. But I don't want to get the old people's discount or be hired as an intern, which is a despicable way to hire experienced professionals, as I discuss in the chapter on not being a sage.

Sometimes your side hustle gives you so much confidence, you end up working for a company as an appropriately paid, respected employee or contractor. You keep up your side hustle as career insurance.

The Bottom Line

When you're engaged in meaningful work, bringing in money at market rates, you may not feel the need to bring forth your inner bitch. You'll be recognized as successful. You'll be proud, strong, and happy. You'll still experience age discrimination, but you can laugh at those insults, all the way to the bank.

Chapter 11:
"Time to Retire The R-Word: Retirement"

"A junior monk asked the abbot, 'When does a fellow get to retire around here?' Pointing to the cemetery, the abbot replied, 'When he's over there.'" — Brother Benet Twedten, OSB, *View from A Monastery*.

"What fuels widespread fears at this moment isn't aging. It's retirement." - Chris Farrell in *Unretirement*.

Once I was invited to be a podcast guest, to talk about starting a business.

My bio included: "Former college professor, now working on the Internet…"

The host helpfully changed my words to, "She retired from teaching…"

I didn't see myself as retiring from anything. In fact, after leaving full-time academia, I taught a few courses online here and there. And I still teach my own courses to people who sign up and pay me.

She talked about how we view the world differently "at our age.' I didn't have the heart to tell her I'm still grounded in attitudes and lifestyles that few would describe as "mature."

There's a widespread belief that age and retirement go together.

Joan Chittister, a Benedictine nun, wrote a popular book that purports to question common notions of aging, but in fact reinforces many stereotypes.

She's right when she asks about "a culture that begins to eliminate its experienced workers at the age of fifty-five on the basis of a stereotype which does not hold up under scrutiny, but which is very difficult to change." (p. 22)

Chittister encourages raging "against the dying of the light," referencing the Dylan Thomas poem. But here are her examples of those who are raging:

Ed, late eighties, plays "at least nine holes of golf" before going to "the club."

Bud, seventies, plays cards and tells jokes every afternoon.

Kathleen, nearly ninety, works in charities every day because "everybody wanted her."

Tim, "over eighty," was "the highest rated volunteer in Meals on Wheels."

Ted, "high seventies," a former banker and financial manager now consults with nonprofits.

"No stereotype here," Chittister says

Ironically, her examples show just how deeply the stereotypes have been normalized. These five people aren't working in careers where they can earn money, let alone market wages. They're playing the stereotype retirement games -- volunteer work, nonprofits, cards, and golf.

Later in her book, Chittister writes about retirement:

"The work we do after we retire is not useless, valueless work simply because it is not paid labor... these years are for the development of the soul. These are the years we learn to paint, or go back to playing an instrument again, or become a Little League coach, or visit nursing homes so that the people there, so many of them alone in the world, have someone to talk to about important things."

Yet the biggest challenge for many people after sixty-five isn't *choosing* to work at something meaningful. It's overcoming the belief that, at your age, you're no longer interested in competing for market-level rewards. It's overcoming the belief that only unpaid, charitable, benevolent work will be "meaningful" once you reach the official "retirement age."

The R-word is a new one.

As Chris Farrell points out in his book *Unretirement*, (p. 4), retirement is "a relatively new lifestyle for elder Americans... a post-World War II phenomenon."

If I ran the world, we would retire the word "retirement." We would talk about shifting gears in our working life. We might talk about stepping back from work to live a dream.

Gisela, a veterinarian in her late thirties, took a leave of absence from her practice with the goal of hiking in the Rocky Mountains - something that she'd always dreamed of. She loved her profession and her practice, but she wanted to make time for a dream. She might return to her current practice, move somewhere else or even find a new career.

Robert made a lot of money with a big tech company. After he left, in his thirties, he never got around to looking for a new job in the same industry. He became a fitness trainer and Zumba teacher. Eventually, he was invited to manage an upscale fitness center at a hotel - a low-key job he loved.

Harold was laid off from his information systems job in his mid-fifties. Even before the pandemic, he had worked remotely, and he had developed a passionate interest in ceramics. He realized he didn't need to work. His husband contributed to the household expenses, and he'd accumulated a fair amount of savings.

He decided not to look for another job. Instead, he spent massive amounts of time in a ceramics studio, making art that he could eventually sell.

Harold could say he retired. But he sees himself as transitioning from information systems to art. He doesn't need to describe his work as part-time or full-time. He can work as many hours as he needs to earn the level of income he desires. Period.

You can refuse to retire ... ever.

John Leland describes an eighty-six-year-old who's still working as an artist. He doesn't have many friends his own age.

Then there's Florence Rigney, a 94-year-old operating room nurse working shifts at the Tacoma General Hospital in Washington. "While she's probably the oldest working nurse in the world, colleagues say that they sometimes struggle to keep up with her," writes Frieda Paton in NursesLabs.

Rigney cut back to two days a week. Rather than assist at operations, she prepares the room and the patient. Still, she stays current with technology. She learned how to use a computer.

You could call Florence Rigney "semi-retired." But why not say she's reached a point in her life when she's able to choose her hours — and she got lucky choosing her merry-go-round?

After you reach a certain age, work isn't work anymore. It's "not retired."

Go for a search on Amazon. What demographic group has the most career guides?

You'll find few if any career guides for Black people or gay people.

You'll find lots of career guides for women in all career stages, often using "high heels" or "stilettos" as the iconic image of career success. My feet hurt just thinking about it.

"Career guide for retirement age" outnumbers them all.

Clearly, the publishing world sees a demand for books on helping people consciously replace traditional retirement with jobs. They almost always encourage their readers to replace market-level income with the satisfaction of "leaving a legacy."

The term "encore career" has caught on ... and it's dangerous.

Marc Freedman wrote a book defining encore careers as the approach most appropriate for those who want to keep working as they get older. The term has become so popular, it's used in mainstream media without referencing Freedman at all.

At first, the term "encore careers" sounds appealing. Inherently it's ageist.

When do performers offer encores? After the performance is over. Encores are never part of the main show. They're light-hearted songs or musical numbers, designed for the audience to walk out smiling.

Most important, encores aren't spontaneous. They're carefully planned. Audience members believe they're getting extra value for their ticket price.

Is that the metaphor we want to use for later-life careers? Something extra, tacked on at the end, that nobody takes seriously?

I'm not buying any of it.

Chris Farrell's book on career options after aging is called *Unretirement*. Ironically, this title further reinforces the stereotype: after a certain age, you're defined as "retired" or "not retired." Or you're "still working"

You're not allowed to identify as simply "working."

But he goes on to say (p. 9), "If the popular images of retirement are the golf course and the RV, the defining institutions of unretirement are the workplace and the entrepreneurial start-up."

Later in his book, Farrell acknowledges, "The barriers to unretirement are formidable and change won't come overnight. Far too many employers are hostile to the idea of hiring someone with gray hair." (p. 92)

True, it's in their interest to claim it's "normal" for "older" people to retire, so now you're excused if you choose to discriminate openly.

If you see a ten-year-old out playing at 10 AM, it's perfectly appropriate to ask, "Shouldn't you be in school?" If you see a professional woman over 65 attending a business event, it's absolutely not appropriate to ask, "Shouldn't you be retired?"

Working brings you more than money. MUCH more.

When you say you're retired, a few people will envy you. But mostly you'll be taken less seriously.

"You don't mind waiting for the doctor, do you? After all, you're retired and this guy's got a flight to catch."

Researchers Wu, Odden et al. found that people who retire early are more likely to die sooner. One possible explanation: sick people retire earlier. Their research study met this claim head-on, finding those who delayed retirement had lower all-cause mortality rates (i.e., regardless of the reason for dying), whether they were healthy or unhealthy.

Writing in the APA Monitor, Jamie Chamberlin quotes several studies that question the value of retirement. The Sloan Center on Aging and Work and the Families and Work Institute issued a report in 2010, "Working in Retirement: A 21st Century Phenomenon." This Report found that 20% of "workers" enjoy a post-retirement job while 75% expect to move to a post-retirement second career.

Furthermore, the Report suggests, retirees who continued working reported "levels of health, well-being and life satisfaction on par with those who have not yet retired - despite age differences."

Let's replace "retirement" with "career transition."

If you're an airline pilot, a football player, a ballet dancer, a police officer, or a member of the military, you know you'll eventually leave your career with no possibility of return. That's forced retirement and you knew the rules when you signed on.

In other fields, you may be forced out by changes in your company or industry. You may wake up one day and say, "I cannot face getting up and going to work at this job anymore."

You might have health issues that force a change - at any age. Imagine being a 35-year-old veterinarian who becomes allergic to latex.

There's no reason to link these events to age. They're inevitable in any career. You'll need a new dream and as much money as you can save.

Don't save for retirement. Save for a dream.

Financial planners like to ask, "How are you saving for retirement?"

Why not ask instead, "What is your dream and how are you working to fund it?"

Follow up with...

"What would be an ideal lifestyle for you? Do you want to do the whole 'take this job and shove it' thing? Do you want to live in a warm climate and work a few hours a day from your deck? Do you want to take a couple of years and travel? Do you want to go back to school and get a degree?"

These questions will be much more meaningful than, "When do you want to retire?"

After all, it's not about age. It's about financial wealth, freedom from family obligations, motivation, mindset, and health. That could happen as early as age 35 or as late as "never."

Want to focus on a specific dream? Think "sabbatical."

Back in the mid-nineties, I got incredibly lucky: I was able to take a year off, due to a quirky university terminal sabbatical policy. I was living in Philadelphia, where I live now. I decided to use the time to learn about art and music, so I spent a lot of time going to art museums and concerts.

I also decided not to worry about money during this time. I had savings and a small income from the university. However, I did do some adjunct teaching at a local university, and I had a contract to write my book on moving, which was published as *Making the Big Move*.

By the end of the year, I had a new job and a book ready for publication. The time off was meaningful and at times almost magical…but I was ready to go back to work.

Your sabbatical may or may not coincide with saying good-by to your career. "I'm going on a sabbatical" sounds a lot more positive than "I'm heading for retirement."

To make a sabbatical work, you need a goal. What will you do with your time? What would make you look back on this time and say, "I got what I came for?"

If you've come to a crossroads in your career, a sabbatical will give you a chance to fulfill a very specific, time-bounded dream. You may find that you walk away with a clearer understanding of what you'd like to do next.

In fact, a sabbatical can lead to a whole new lifestyle. In their late thirties, Betsy and Warren Talbot sold their Seattle home to travel for a year. They never came back. Many years later, they're permanently relocated overseas after developing an online business that allows them to live anywhere while enjoying a comfortable income.

If they'd started at age 65, they'd be stereotyped as "retired."

Transitioning to New Careers

Throughout most of your life, you're advised to avoid "leaving from." You're supposed to think of "moving to" something. If you don't have a new destination, you're advised to stay where you are till you have a plan.

Then comes retirement, which is 100% "leaving from." So many people make the leap, we see hundreds of books, workshops, classes, and coaching offers to deal with problems of retirement: boredom, loss of purpose, loss of identity, loss of status, and yes, loss of money.

A whole cottage industry of books and groups has emerged to shepherd people - especially women - through the "transition" from prime years of employment to retirement alternatives. For instance, The Transition Network, with branches in several cities, supports women over fifty who meet in groups of 10-12 in their homes.

The Network defines its members as highly accomplished women who find they have "no blueprint for moving from one life stage to another." As they say on their website, "The idea of retiring at age 65 as an 'old person' no longer made sense." In 2000, the founders set out to create just such a blueprint.

The Network is premised on beliefs about circumstances shared by women as they age. For many women, joining an age-based group will be rewarding. The programming seems to support not only career and business questions, but also medical concerns ("is a mammogram enough") and information on wills and trusts.

Some people wear retirement like a badge.

They love saying, "I'm retired." They proudly proclaim, "I worked hard. I earned the money. I can do it."

There's just one catch.

A lot of people who proudly define themselves as "retired" find themselves sneaking back into work where they get paid market rates.

Willow, a licensed psychologist, spent a few years traveling with her newly-retired husband. He'd worked for one of those demanding companies with a beyond-generous retirement plan. She didn't have to go back to work, ever.

For a few years, her friends got postcards and social media posts from exotic locations around the world.

Then one day I got an email, "I'm jumping through hoops to get my license transferred to my new state. I want to go back to work."

Why not? She was in her sixties. She's in a field where she can work as long as she can fulfill her responsibilities to her clients. Some clients will even seek out an "older" therapist.

The one thing that needs to be retired is the word Retirement.

I'd rather spend a day in a coworking space than in a senior center, anytime.

Chapter 12: "Volunteering Should Be Voluntary at Any Age"

"Legacy is a stupid thing! I don't want a legacy." - Bill Gates

Many years ago, when I was living in San Francisco, I volunteered with the SPCA. I still remember the first lesson from our orientation.

The Volunteer Coordinator asked why we were volunteering. We talked about having fun and wanting to play with the animals.

Rather than expressing dismay at our frivolous, "I'm in this for me" answers, she applauded. The best volunteers, she said, are the selfish volunteers. They want to gain something for themselves. They don't come in talking about how to make a difference.

It's part of the aging stereotype: Old = Volunteer

The story goes like this. Older people are supposed to be retired. They have time on their hands. More importantly, they want to leave a legacy. They want to do things that will help others.

Volunteering also gets touted as a way to compensate for the rewards of paid labor. For example, Jennifer Crittenden, an administrator with the University of Maine Center on Aging, says volunteering lets people "replace lost roles" after retirement.

That's fine if you want to give up those roles. If you genuinely enjoy volunteering, go for it. I totally admire the wonderful people of all ages who volunteer to work in animal rescue. A mixed-age group cares for our local park, doing the weeding and planting that's beyond the city's budget. Countless Philadelphians of all ages work with children to enhance their reading and writing skills.

The problem comes when "growing older" and "volunteering" are supposed to go together, just like "growing older" and "retired." With this logic, "growing older" somehow rules out the possibility of "continuing to work at market rates in a competitive field."

"We won't consider hiring anyone over 60. You'd be so much happier being a volunteer, wouldn't you?"

Maybe you would. But I want the opportunity to say, "No, thank you. I'd rather make money and donate to my charities. Let the professionals do the work instead of some half-baked amateur like me."

Volunteering doesn't come cheap.

Volunteering often means you can afford to forego paid employment. You most likely incur expenses for travel and meals. In fact, "older adults" sometimes stop volunteering because they need funds.

Volunteering doesn't guarantee you'll make a difference.

Crittenden notes that "many communities have more potential older volunteers than they can effectively deploy." You might arrive at your place of volunteering, only to end up standing around, feeling useless.

She thinks it's a matter of matching people to jobs. More likely, we're putting too much emphasis on volunteer work as a way for "older" people to solve problems from alleviating loneliness to gaining a sense of purpose.

First, I haven't seen any research comparing the ways older people benefit from volunteer work vs. professional work paid at market rates.

And secondly, maybe we don't need all those volunteers after all. One of the most depressing experiences a volunteer can have is to show up, eager to serve, only to realize she's not needed.

Over the years, I've tried volunteering.

I have been a volunteer usher with theatres to get free admission, even when I could easily afford a ticket. If the show's a bummer, I feel better if I didn't shell out fifty dollars. I enjoy talking to the other volunteers and audience members during intermission.

But I admit I'm not the world's greatest usher. I've been known to forget to tear off ticket stubs and send people to the wrong rows. I forget where I'm supposed to be standing.

I've also been a volunteer tour guide in Philadelphia. I wanted to learn the city's history and the guides were a fun group of all ages.

Mostly I enjoyed guiding and gave a pretty good tour, but I had just one problem. I have a very poor sense of direction. Luckily, every tour had at least one local person who could say tactfully, "Isn't Independence Hall over there?" Or, "I think we just passed Macy's."

Work with animals? Depending on the rescue agency, you can make a huge difference. Most animal charities rely heavily on volunteers.

I tried. I patted the cats. They escaped from their cages and the kennel attendant had to chase after them and put them back.

I walked some dogs. They pulled so hard they knocked me over.

Eventually, I contributed by writing blurbs for the adoption websites until they changed the system.

I enjoyed those experiences while I did them. But they're extra - the frosting on the cake. For me, volunteering won't compensate for the rewards and stimulation of paid work.

Nice Means "Being Willing to Work for Nothing"

A Huffington Post article raises the question: Should We Stop Being Nice to Older Adults? The author, Dr. Roger Landry, gets off to a nice start - emphasizing that treating older people as somehow disabled or needy doesn't help. But apparently "nice" seems to mean, "being willing to work for nothing." A new version of Miss Congeniality.

In his article, Landry helpfully suggests four roles for older people. All of them amount to drafting us into low-paid servant roles.

"What if our older Americans were expected to become part of our education system?" he asks.

Well, why not? Why can't we take jobs as teachers and administrators and get paid market rates?

I'd be happy to serve as an educator … but I'd want to be recognized and paid for my skills. I'm neither qualified for, nor interested in, working with children. I'd be delighted to serve on a university faculty...and not just as an underpaid, undervalued, disposable adjunct. I'm happy to offer courses online and charge market rates. I don't feel like donating my time and hard-earned knowledge just because I'm "older."

Or what about getting "experienced and motivated grandparents" into our "childcare system?" Landry asks.

Associating "older adults" with "childcare" reinforces the stereotypes of aging. As soon as you reach your sixties you suddenly get an urge to knit booties and kiss babies.

Marc Freedman wrote a book, *How to Live Forever*, about the value of mixing the generations. Sounds like a great idea, but he seems to suggest the older generation should play a nurturing role while the younger generation gets a free ride.

When Freedman's three children need someone to watch over them, he can't turn to his own parents; they live too far away. Instead, he writes, "Our silver-haired safety net is located two doors down. Our quirky, engaging eighty-something neighbors …have become quasi-grandparents for our children… "

Wait just a minute. Does that mean they're unpaid babysitters? Should they be honored to be called a "silver-haired safety net?" Try saying "our brown-skinned safety net." Or "our gay pride safety net." If you didn't find those terms offensive, just wait and someone will (rightly) tell you so.

Back to Landry, who further suggests "a registry of skilled older adults who were ready to mentor or act as consultants to businesses and organizations."

We already have something like this in the United States through the Small Business Administration. I've heard stories from grateful business owners who say, "I couldn't have started my business without them."

But frankly, being a business consultant is a valuable skill. If people can't afford to hire paid help, they can apply for grants, take courses or decide they're not ready to become an entrepreneur just yet.

Would you volunteer for a suicide mission?

If you're going to draft older people, why not draft us into the military for undercover suicide missions? Make that an option for people with terminal cancer or Alzheimer's. If I had an incurable disease, I'd rather go down in flames -- literally -- than end my days lying in a bed, dealing with needles, tubes, and insensitive caregivers. I'd love to be remembered as a heroine who died fighting for a worthy cause.

Alas, when I presented this idea to an active-duty soldier, he pointed out that the military rarely plans suicide missions these days. If they change their minds, some of us are ready to enlist.

Why not get paid for leaving a legacy?

I've left a very nice legacy while getting paid as a business school professor and later as a marketing consultant. People tell me I helped change their lives when they were students, readers, or clients. One woman wrote, "I carried your relocation book with me during my cross-country move. I took it out and read a little every night and it really helped."

I know my limits. I'm not a kindly old lady filled with sympathy. You want me to save the world? You can pay me for my services, and I'll donate to a real professional who can do some good where it counts.

Chapter 13: "Take this pill and shove it"

"Medicine's much hailed ability to help the sick is fast being challenged by its propensity to harm the healthy". – R. Moynihan, J. Doust and C. Henry. BMJ 2012.

"No pills? You're not a real person."

You already know I'm not a doctor, right? My Ph.D. is in marketing. I'm qualified to spot a scam a mile away, but not to advise you on your medical decisions.

Once you reach a certain age, doctors stop asking, "Are you taking any meds?" Instead, they ask, "*What* medications are you taking?"

Their intake forms leave space for at least a hundred. There's no place to check off "none."

No wonder blood pressure goes up as people get older. They have more to fight against every time they see a doctor.

"Keep going...we'll find something."

To a healthy person, doctor visits feel like a scavenger hunt: how many reasons for testing can they come up with in the next 5 minutes?

When I moved to Philadelphia, I made the mistake of signing up for a Medicare Advantage program - the kind where you need a

Personal Care Physician (PCP) to be your gatekeeper. My friend recommended an outstanding PCP. Unfortunately, he had stopped taking new patients.

When I injured my shoulder, the only doctor available was a newly graduated, well-dressed young woman who looked about twelve years old. She was eager to practice everything she'd learned in medical school. Ignoring my arm (which had turned coal-black) she asked earnestly, "Do you have problems with earwax?"

"You fell! You probably have balance problems." (I tripped while carrying an awkward load with 2 laptops. One laptop fell on my arm. Ouch!)

These tests could add ten years to your life." (Are you serious?)

As I left, she ran after me yelling, "Are you sure you don't want bloodwork?"

Was she practicing medicine or selling used cars? I resisted giving her the finger.

By the time I got to a desperately needed x-ray, she'd gone home. The x-ray people (not wanting to share their findings with a mere patient) sent me home without telling me the arm was fractured.

The PCP wasn't concerned with helping me find an orthopedic specialist. I had to get on the phone myself and call around. Begging might be a better word.

At the time I didn't know the system for finding a medical specialist. You don't call a specialist directly; you find someone who was a godparent to the specialist's favorite child who will make the call for you. Otherwise, you hear, "If you can wait six months…"

The well-groomed PCP did leave a joyful message. "Aha! Since you have a fracture, you need a bone density test."

I started researching bone density tests. There's a good chapter in the book *Seeking Sickness* and a thoroughly terrifying article from NPR, "How a Bone Disease Grew to Fit the Prescription."

When I finally found an orthopedic specialist, she set me straight. "Don't bother with the test. The medicine is awful. You're in good shape so you'll heal fast and regain your mobility."

And so I did.

"Because you're old" can lead to cruel and deadly medical interventions.

In their June 13-14 issue, *The Wall Street Journal* titled their leading editorial - the one in the upper left, with extra-large type - "The Covid Age Penalty." The article began, "By now it's clear that people older than 65 are the most vulnerable to the novel coronavirus."

There was just one problem: They presented no evidence that age alone makes people more susceptible to getting the virus or experiencing more severe illness. Older people do represent a high percentage of Covid19 deaths. But none of the media bothered to break down the numbers by "pre-existing conditions" and "resident of a nursing home."

Less than 5% of people over 65 reside in nursing homes, yet nursing homes accounted for 42% to 45% of US deaths from Covid. As I write in my chapter on prisons, nursing homes have been spreading disease and infection for years. People in nursing homes can't be compared to active people.

Ironically, the WSJ itself published an article showing that these age effects did not hold in Mexico; younger people tended to have just as many comorbidities and few older people live in nursing homes.

Even more ironically, the article headlined "Age Penalty" contained these words, buried deeply below the headline: "The good news is that most people over 65 who are in generally good health are unlikely to die or get severely ill from COVID-19."

At an early stage of the pandemic, California's Governor Newsom encouraged the state's five million seniors to remain home, not even venturing out to grocery stores.

According to a report from laist.com, in what has to be one of the major understatements of the pandemic, "Newsom recognized that asking millions of seniors to stay home was bound to create anxiety." He promised his team would work on "services to help these seniors with food and medication."

In response, one reader wrote: "I am a very healthy, active 65-year-old woman...Being outdoors is good for us. I need to walk my three dogs, and the walk is good for me, too. I don't need to go near anyone. I love to garden—at least that's one thing I can do with all this time alone."

"Orwell's 1984 is here."

What's even scarier is that some "experts" justified age-based lockdowns to maximize economic outcomes and limit the virus. NBER (National Bureau of Economic Research) projected outcomes of placing restrictions only on people over 65.

"The 65-and-over group has 20 percent of the earnings of the younger groups and, crucially, faces a much higher mortality rate from COVID-19,' said NBER. Therefore, they recommended easing up on restrictions for the under-65 crowd while "those over 65 remain under complete lockdown until the arrival of a vaccine."

As with Newsom's policy, it's not clear how those in "complete lockdown" would get food, medical care, and recreation. And these policies completely ignore the majority of people in that group who enjoy good health and want to stay that way.

A dose of ageism, delivered with your health care

An article in *Health Leaders Media* notes that 1 in 5 American adults report age discrimination in health care settings. For example, doctors may refuse to treat symptoms they claim are natural features of aging; conversely, they treat thes "natural effect of aging" as a disease. Medical staff "may share ageist jokes or may [unconsciously] have implicit ageist thoughts and behaviors toward elderly patients..."

As usual, the comments on that article are more explicit and more colorful.

"I hear stories of [doctors] saying, you're old what do you expect, or you should be thankful you're passed your expiry date."

"The world has moved doctors into the same place as a used car salesman or lawyer."

"I am past retirement age and work full time. I have no physical challenges yet [in a medical setting] was asked over and over if I have assistance getting around at home. The nurses didn't bother reading the previous notes and one asked the question a least four times. Each nurse asked if I have fallen in the last two years... I told one nurse, 'Not even when shoveling the snow out of my driveway.'"

It's not your imagination: some doctors really don't like older people.

In his excellent book, *What Your Doctor Won't Tell You About Getting Older*, geriatrician Mark Lachs has no qualms about calling out the bad apples in the medical profession. One doctor actually removed chairs from his consulting room so elderly patients wouldn't be tempted to stick around and ask questions.

Louise Aronson, in her book *Elderhood*, shares a story about a hospital resident who was summoned to admit a dying person. Assuming the patient was old, he allocated fifteen minutes to her. Just another old person, right?

Later he found out the woman was in her forties. His response was, "If I'd known she was younger, I'd have allocated more time. We need to show the age more prominently on charts."

Another time, Aronson says, a woman called an ambulance for her aging mother. "She's old and this is the middle of the night," the angry attendant said. "What do you expect?"

As a true bitchy broad, I always call attention to my fitness when I visit a doctor.

"Get on the scale? You must be kidding. Do I look like I've got a weight problem? No? Good. Let's move on."

"I don't get these muscles by being a couch potato."

"I'm probably more fit than half the people in this office." (My eye doctor responded sardonically, "Only half?")

Obnoxious? Sure. Do they call me a bitch? Probably. Do I care? Hell, no.

These moments keep me going whenever I'm tempted to skip a workout.

Doctors say you're lucky to see a doctor at all.

In the US, once you reach sixty-five, you must go on Medicare. No choice. Medicare pays doctors at a negotiated rate. Depending on the doctor's relationship with Medicare, you may or may not be able to pay extra.

Some doctors simply refuse to see Medicare patients. Period. The Health Information Council reports that the percentage of doctors refusing Medicare remains small but growing. Nearly 10,000 doctors left Medicare in 2012.

By March of 2020, that number was up to 26,000. Forty percent of the opt-outs are psychiatrists.

The Medicare system helps millions of Americans, yet also sets them up to be viewed as second-rate patients. If you experience chronic conditions requiring frequent visits to a primary care physician, you might opt for concierge care. If you're healthy, concierge care won't make sense for you.

When you visit a doctor with your Medicare card, your doctor quickly realizes you are not going to be a cash cow. Quick visits for the bare minimum you need? You're a nuisance.

Maybe you're better off with less medicine.

On the other hand, you may be better off staying away from doctors. As reported by NPR, a 2003 study by Elliott Fisher compared Medicare patients with comparable levels of sickness across the United States. In some places, the "elderly" people used fewer health care services; in others, they used considerably more.

"The patients in the high-spending regions were getting about 60 percent more care; 60 percent more days in the hospital; twice as many specialist visits," Fisher says. "And yet when we followed patients for up to five years, if you lived in one of these higher-intensity communities, your survival [rate] was certainly no better, and in many cases a little bit worse."

Once a doctor said to me (carefully lowering his voice), "The reason you're so healthy is you've avoided doctors." Genes help but I definitely feel I've dodged a bullet.

Medical ageism starts early.

Geriatrician Mark Lachs points out that medical ageism doesn't start at sixty-five. In his 40s, he sought medical advice for an injured toe. The doctor dismissed his concerns, saying something along the lines of, "Just buddy-tape the toes. You're not going to be an Olympic athlete."

Replace medical ageism with medical freedom.

A certified Aging Bitch will do everything possible to choose medical providers who won't force her to undergo unnecessary tests. They won't reference everything in terms of age. She'll do her homework. She'll realize that, like many aspects of life, "less is more" is the best approach to medical care.

I am not a doctor (as I've said many times). I believe you can fight for medical freedom with every visit. I won't accept bullying from doctors who insist on tests and procedures that can be justified only by the revenue they bring to the hospitals. I'm well aware of options to report doctors to state medical boards and even their own hospitals. (In case you're wondering, I also write complimentary letters when I find good doctors. It doesn't happen often.)

Dealing with the medical system? You have to be willing to be seen as a bitch.

Doctors come to your visit with prejudices, biases, and a lack of information. Sometimes they come with just plain greed.

When you're admitted to something that looks like a hospital room, you might be tempted to say, "Of course I'm an in-patient in a hospital." But you might actually be in a category of "under observation."

The hospital uses the category to avoid getting penalized for high re-admission rates. You get penalized because you get reimbursed under different Medicare programs, leaving you with a higher deductible and a change in your eligibility to be covered for follow-up care.

Medicare patients are supposed to be notified of their status within 36 hours. That's a lot of hours and there is no appeal. Ideally, you are supposed to take the initiative to ask about your status before you agree to be admitted...even though you might not be conscious.

How's that for building trust?

You can't be Miss Congeniality.

I love my current eye doctor. But many of the female techs show up with long, pointy fingernails. I'm not letting their ungloved fingers come anywhere near my eyes. When a tech said, "You have to let me do this," I replied, "No I don't. I can refuse. You just write in your chart, 'Patient refused procedure.'"

She wasn't happy. The doctor sighed and said he'd personally take a look at her fingernails. Sixteen years of education for this?

When I showed up for cataract surgery, (with my former eye doctor) the hospital - a world-renowned facility- kept me waiting. Finally, a tech showed up. She said, "We have to hurry. We're running late." I pointed out that I'd been there since way before my appointment.

I went along with the process. I should have stopped and demanded to see her supervisor. People in a hurry make mistakes.

When I told the doctor I didn't see as well with my left eye, she lied blatantly. She said, "It's the drugs."

I changed doctors. I wrote them up on public forums. I wrote to the hospital, which ignored me.

It's terrifying to think of the incompetence and callousness of these medical professionals. We have to fight the stereotype every day.

If you set a priority of "being nice," you might find an appreciative doctor who goes the extra mile for you.

Or you might find they see you as easy pickings.

To protect yourself, do three things.

Report problems.

An Aging Bitch will not hesitate to fight for her health. She'll write letters to her legislators. She'll complain to medical people, hospitals, and regulatory agencies. Sometimes she'll be ignored. When enough people are willing to complain, things will change.

After my encounter with the injured arm, I wrote a long, detailed letter to the Chief of Staff of the Medical Service.

When I read those ridiculous pre-op requirements for lid surgery, I wrote the Chief Ophthalmologist of the clinic.

In both cases, I got a detailed, thoughtful reply. One was sensible; one wasn't. But they answered.

Imagine what would happen if they got 100 letters a week. They might actually consider making some overdue changes.

Clarify your values.

In 2014, a bioethicist named Ezekiel Emanuel published a controversial article in the *Atlantic Monthly*: Why I Hope To Die At 75.

Emanuel, a physician on the faculty of the University of Pennsylvania, doesn't support assisted dying. Instead, he urges skipping the diagnostic tests and treatment for diseases that occur naturally.

He points out that extending our lives often means extending the years we suffer from pain, loss of mobility, and mental deterioration. Sure, dying is tragic, but so are years spent in misery, often waiting to die.

He paints a gloomy picture:

"The American immortal, once a vital figure in his or her profession and community, is happy to cultivate avocational interests, to take up bird watching, bicycle riding, pottery, and the like. And then, as walking becomes harder and the pain of arthritis limits the fingers' mobility, life comes to center around sitting in the den reading or listening to books on tape and doing crossword puzzles."

He explains:

"[At 75] I will stop getting any regular preventive tests, screenings, or interventions. I will accept only palliative—not curative—treatments if I am suffering pain or other disability."

That's a rare example of a value-based decision, from a physician, no less. He's careful to say that most people won't agree with him and that's okay.

Some people will decide they want to live as long as possible, no matter what it takes. Caretakers? Nursing homes? They'll make the tradeoff.

Others will ask questions like, "OK, so you'll cure me of heart disease...but then I'll get cancer. No cancer? I'll be at risk for dementia if I live long enough."

Another value system might be, "After 75 I won't resist a quick way to die. Pneumonia and flu are preferable to cancer or heart disease."

Still another might be, "I want to decide when I die, even if I'm healthy. I'd rather cut off years of life to avoid spending time with dementia or living in a bed at the mercy of a nursing home."

To establish values, you have to know the facts. If you get cured of one condition, will you be more vulnerable to something worse? If you avoid treatment, will you be condemned to a life of misery?"

Be your own medical detective.

Many doctors want to help their patients get the best results. However, you should be aware they often don't have time to dig into the research. They're usually far too busy seeing patients and entering data into their EMRs. They mostly rely on guidelines and, occasionally, "what everybody knows."

And they read selectively.

They read guidelines suggesting prescriptions for osteopenia, which is said to be the early phase of osteoporosis. They don't even see an investigative article by NPR showing that osteopenia was actually invented by the Merck drug company

They make sure your record has a place for BMI. Who cares? Writing in the journal *iScience*, Glenn A. Gaesser and Siddhartha S. Angadi report: "Epidemiological studies show that cardiorespiratory fitness and physical activity significantly attenuate, and sometimes eliminate, the increased mortality risk associated with obesity."

In plain English: Being fit will usually compensate for being fat.

Unfortunately, it's not always easy to get the facts.

For instance, it seems reasonable to ask, "What percentage of people with high blood pressure actually get heart disease?" When I googled this question, I found statistics from the American Heart Association showing that 77% percent of people with heart attacks also had high blood pressure.

That's called the post hoc hoc fallacy. It's like the example used in countless statistics classes. Most people who use hard drugs started with marijuana. But it's not true that most marijuana users graduate to hard drugs.

Best to stay away from the chirpy-cheery articles with the party line. Look up books and articles that tell it like it is. Armed with this knowledge, you ask questions before you accept a diagnosis or prescription. If necessary, you seek a second opinion.

And don't feel bad if you overhear them saying as you leave, "Let's hope that bitch finds another doctor next time." You deserve better.

Chapter 14: "Forget my age. I still kick some serious butt."

"Even for athletes, the effect of age on performance is far less consequential than once believed." - [Jeff Haden in *Inc. Magazine.*]

"Elder is a life phase.... that's great. Being ill, that's hard. That's a disease. They're not the same. We tend to think that they're one and the same." - Steve Petrow, quoted in a Next Avenue interview.

Here's another word association test.

Say "old."

You'll get a response like, "Sick." Or "Frail." Or even, "Helpless."

We're trained to think that way.

Every bus in Philadelphia designates certain seats "for the elderly and disabled." I've always liked sitting upfront, even when I was a teen, so I sit there. I feel a little guilty when I'm wearing shorts and a tee, bound for my Zumba class.

Try typing "Old and ... " into a search engine.

"Old and inform." "Old and disabled." "Old and lonely." "Old and demented."

Earlier I quoted the *New Yorker* article, where Arthur Krystal defines old age as a series of physical ailments, concluding, "Not surprisingly, sixty-eight percent of Medicare beneficiaries today have multiple chronic conditions."

It's enough to make anyone feel, well, sick.

What's even worse: If you don't relate to this description, you have no place in the health care system. The only way you can survive is to risk being labeled "that bitch."

Health problems are real.

If you have significant ongoing health problems, you deserve respectful treatment. The "old equals sick" stereotype hurts you, too.

All too many doctors treat their patients based on what they believe about "most people."

"You think you're healthy, but you really need a cardiologist..."

My eyelids were drooping over my eyes, obstructing my side vision. My eye doctor suggested surgery for a lift as medically necessary. Insurance would probably cover it.

There was just one problem. I needed pre-op clearance. Half a dozen articles show that pre-op clearance doesn't make a bit of difference for this type of surgery. Never mind. Medical centers read research only when it suits their purposes. They want clearance.

Since I'm on the Ezekiel Emanuel plan, and a reader of *Less Medicine More Health*, I don't do screenings. Research shows annual physical exams produce little benefit. Why bother?

Now I'm forced to go into the belly of the beast - the world of primary care - to get a signature.

One doctor asked me how old I was. When I told him, he began sputtering, "No, no, no. I can't be responsible. You need to see a cardiologist."

Let's get this straight. I'm doing everything you're supposed to do. I exercise and I'm seriously fit. I'm a 40-year meditator. I eat healthy food (with some cheating for ice cream, bacon, and chocolate). No meds.

The head anesthesiologist admitted – in writing – that the "system" isn't designed for healthy people. I know what I'd like to design for the system.

Doctors make decisions based on "most people..."

Be prepared for doctors to look at one number on your chart - your age - instead of looking at you.

I've heard about a poster in a doctor's office with fifty tests you need when you reach fifty. Each test represents a big *ka-ching!* for the cash register.

Big Pharma needs older people to blame every ache and pain on old age. "See a PT and do some stretches" won't sell pain meds like "Everybody over sixty has back pain."

Doctors ignore variance.

When your doctor says, "Most older people have high blood pressure," or, "Most older people have trouble sleeping," she may be right.

But we know for certain that the variance among older people is huge. The gap grows as we get older.

We have lots of 80-year-olds living miserably in so-called care homes, barely able to walk. And then we have Willie Murphy, the 82-year-old who broke a table on the burglar who dared to invade her home.

Even worse, statistics on "older people" often include nursing home residents. Nursing homes can make their residents sicker. Their doctor decides you need treatment for a disease, even though you'll probably be dead before that disease gets serious enough to make a difference.

Many institutions won't let you refuse medical care. You can't argue that you'd rather die of a heart attack than take a handful of pills that weaken your muscles so you can't walk easily anymore.

A study published in the *European Journal of Ageing* reviewed ageism in the healthcare field. They noted, "Healthcare professionals have a biased experience with older adults because they tend to see and treat only the most frail, sick, and senile older people."

The article notes that nurses tend to have "less accurate knowledge about the aging process" than other medical professionals. Yet nurses are the staff patients encounter most, apart from technicians, who were not mentioned.

The naked truth about medical stereotypes.

A few years ago, I was in my gym's locker room, ready to take a shower, dressed appropriately in a white towel and nothing else. I noticed a woman – probably in her 40s or 50s – openly looking me over. That is very unusual in locker rooms, not to mention a little creepy.

"I'm an Ob-Gyn," the woman explained. "You're in better shape than most of my patients. And they're young."

I didn't know whether to be flattered or insulted. She's calling me fit, but she's also calling me old. But, I figured, it's a one-off encounter. I forgot it.

Fast forward a few years. New gym, same body, also en route to the showers. Another woman is looking me over.

"You're moving easily," she says incredulously. "You don't have pain when you walk, do you? Your joints don't ache?"

"Um, no," I thought, once again feeling like this is creepy.

It turns out she's a geriatric nurse. She works in a hospital. She's never seen a healthy person over sixty.

Older people are not inherently unhealthy.

Christiane Northrup, a board-certified Ob-Gyn, directly attacks these beliefs in her book, *Goddesses Never Age*: "There are people in their 20's who show signs of aging – lower muscle mass, unstable blood sugar, loss of balance - while people in their 70s are 'the picture of health.'"

Writing in the *New England Journal of Medicine*, geriatrician Louise Aronson ridiculed a WSJ article that identified people in their 70s as "bedridden." Very few people in their 70s, she says, are bedridden.

In her book, *Elderhood*, Aronson associates many physiological changes with age. Yet she also points to her experience as physician to a jail population. A 50-year-old inmate on his first incarceration would show "middle age" symptoms commonly associated with his age. A 50-year-old who'd been in jail a long time might have the body of a 70-year-old.

Unfortunately, she doesn't specify which 70-year-old: a Willie Murphy (the 82-year-old bodybuilder) or a frail patient recovering from a heart attack? But she's on the right track.

As Covid19 drew us into quarantine, many medical professionals pontificated about "weaker immune systems" among the elderly. The published research shows otherwise.

A study in *Aging Cell* looked at the immunity levels of "older" people who had built up fitness through long-term cycling. Older cyclists showed markers of stronger immune systems, compared to the younger couch potatoes.

Many other studies suggest that exercise changes the physiology of older people. We haven't seen a large-scale study because (a) it's hard to set up a randomized trial between long-term exercisers and couch potatoes (do you tell people not to exercise?), and (b) it would be hard to get funding since drugs aren't involved.

Some young people are even less healthy.

Even when medical conditions exist - and I don't want to deny the pain that can be real - we have to remember that not all young people live in perfect health.

Ask younger people the question, "How are you?" One says, "I'm getting over a migraine." Another, "I just got a kidney transplant." Or "I've been depressed for the last two weeks. I don't want to do anything."

Don't get me started on insomnia. Doctors assume you have trouble sleeping as soon as you turn fifty.

I've met people of all ages who have trouble sleeping. If I want to annoy them, I point out that I sleep like a log every night, unless the cat wakes me up to demand a midnight snack.

According to an article in *Clinical Sleep Journal*, older people have trouble sleeping when they're stuck in an institution, living mostly indoors with limited options for exercise; when they take a lot of medications; and when they experience physical or mental illness (e.g., depression).

Seems like people of *any* age would have trouble sleeping under those conditions.

Some researchers suggest that blood pressure and "white coat hypertension" increase with age. They often mutter a lot of jargon about stiffening of the arteries. Maybe that's true.

I say it's another consequence of medical ageism. When you're treated based on one number - your age - it's enough to make anyone's blood boil. Where's that factor in the ongoing studies?

Think about it. The staff marks "Retired" under "Employment Status" without asking if you still work. They offer an arm to help you navigate the hallway even if you run marathons and play tennis every day. They call you "Mrs." and ask about your children after you've filled out their forms as "single" and "sorry, just cats." They call you "honey." They say, "Sit there for me."

I've even been asked, "You don't mind waiting an extra hour, do you? We need to squeeze in a patient who's young, male, and working. You've got all the time in the world, don't you?"

I feel my blood pressure rising just remembering these experiences.

Once I was visiting an orthopedic clinic for an exercise injury. I waited forty-five minutes in a crowded, noisy waiting room with television sets blaring daytime programs. When I finally got to an exam room, the tech held out a blood pressure cuff.

"You must be kidding," I said. "If you want to take my blood pressure, you'd better do something about your waiting room."

The tech tried to tell me I had no choice, but I knew better. There's a space on every medical chart, "Patient refuses." I wrote it up on their follow-up feedback form and nobody ever asked me again.

Imagine a foundation offering your doctor a million dollars to find a way to create a pleasant, quiet waiting room and cut the waiting time down to 15 minutes or less. They'd figure it out.

Chapter 15:
"The Other F Words: Friends and Family"

"Loneliness expresses the pain of being alone and solitude expresses the glory of being alone." -Paul Tillich

"You have more control over loneliness than you might think." - Dr. Dilip Jeste, Psychiatry & Neuroscience Professor, UC San Diego, quoted in *Next Avenue*.

During the Christmas season of 2015, the German store chain Edeka aired a commercial that was ultimately seen by millions. An old man (played by British actor Arthur Nightingale) listens to a voicemail from his daughter: the family won't be home for Christmas.

Frustrated and lonely, the old man tells his children he has died. The children interrupt their busy, far-flung lives to return home. Dressed in black and grieving, they are astonished to find their father alive and well. A fire roars in the fireplace while the newly assembled family reunites joyfully over a holiday meal.

This commercial drew mostly sympathetic responses. I say, "Balderdash!" (Well, I'd say something stronger but it's a holiday.)

The old man strikes me as manipulative, selfish, and greedy. He raised his kids to be successful, and they are. Would he rather have them come crawling home, broke and depressed, to occupy this guest room for the next six months?

I'm reminded of comments we often see in online forums when people post how lonely they are and how much they miss their children. Inevitably someone writes back supportively, "Children are so ungrateful these days."

Nobody's entitled.

Try reversing these roles. Suppose an adult child keeps quitting jobs, behaving irresponsibly, and refusing to manage money. They're able-bodied and mentally healthy. They expect the parents to keep subsidizing them and become angry when the parents say, "Enough. Take charge of your life."

Friends are like bank loans.

When you have money and a good credit rating, banks offer to lend you money. That's a cliché.

When you're happy, busy, and confident, you'll attract all kinds of wonderful people into your life.

One of the most common assumptions about aging is that older people are lonely.

This idea is so deeply ingrained, it appears spontaneously, like dandelions on a lawn in summer. For example, best-selling author Bruce Feiler wrote a best-selling book, *Life Is in The Transitions*. For some mysterious reason, he decided to include this gratuitous comment: "As we age, we feel a greater sense of alienation, loneliness, and loss of purpose, and we feel bored."

Speak for yourself, dude.

Are "older people" really lonelier than everybody else?

A study from the National Academies of Science, Engineering and Medicine suggests that one-fourth - 25% - of people over sixty-five experience social isolation. In other words, 75% of people over 65 do *not* experience social isolation.

A blog post on Next Avenue reports a similar statistic: from the Sloan Center on Aging and Work at Boston College: "92 percent of people ages 55 to 64 — and 76 percent of respondents 65 or older — were involved with paid work, volunteering, caregiving or educational activities."

The Wall Street Journal ran an article on December 11, 2018: The Loneliest Generation. Apparently 8.3% of the Baby Boomers and 7.2% of the Silent Generation "reported they often felt lonely." In comparison, 5.6% of Gen Xers and 2.1% of millennials reported they often felt lonely.

These statistics might seem to tell a sad story for older people, but there's only a 1.6% difference between Gen X and the Silent Generation, and only a 2.7% difference between Gen X and the Boomers.

Millennials seem less lonely than boomers (2.1% vs. 8.3%). At the study date of 2014, they ranged in age from 18 to 33.

At that age, they're perfectly placed to be around potential friends. Some will be in college or even high school. Some will be in the military. Some will be in graduate school or in early career stages. Some still live at home.

It's their stage in life, not their age, that makes a difference. Once you leave school and military environments, you're on your own till you start a family. No more group living!

We might even be seeing cohort effects.

Many studies assess loneliness simply by asking, "Are you lonely?" The way people define loneliness will influence their responses. Many older people have been taught to believe, "It's hard to make friends when you're older."

They may report more loneliness than other generations simply because they have learned to describe their feelings as loneliness. They may have grown up in an era when large extended families and neighborhood friendships were the norm.

"No family around? By definition, you're lonely."

The REAL Reasons Older People Might Feel Lonely (And Why Being a Bitch Keeps You Social)

(1) Today's environment tends to isolate people of all ages (and everybody pretends we're still living in the world of 1950s sitcom shows).

We have all sorts of time-saving gadgets, but we're busier than ever. Setting up a coffee date can take three weeks.

Some of us can remember when we'd casually pick up the phone to call a friend, maybe just to say hello. Today almost all of us accept phone calls by appointment only.

Some people won't even phone. They communicate with brief texts and Facebook posts.

We rarely visit each other's homes unless we're family.

And today's biological family will be smaller and more scattered than families of fifty years ago. Ask people where their grown children live. They'll likely name multiple states of the US and even multiple countries.

Then there's the Real Grandma effect. As your children have children, time priorities shift. You'll want to spend more time with the grandchildren.

If you're not a grandma, your friends suddenly become unavailable. Understandably, they focus on raising the next generation.

If those reasons aren't enough, people move. Before cell phones and emails, people stayed in touch with letters and phone calls. Today when people move, they tend to be out of sight, out of mind. You're lucky to get a short exchange of text messages every now and then.

In her book *Social Chemistry*, Melissa King points out that networks shrink naturally over time. You had a group of friends from a job or a neighborhood. You lose touch with them over time. Unless you replenish those networks – which isn't easy to do – you'll naturally arrive in your later years with fewer friends in your life.

There's nothing wrong with you. It's a phenomenon that's cumulative over time.

"I'm not lonely. I just need a ride home from the hospital."

Your friendly neighborhood hospital assumes you've got someone available to stand by to give you a ride home after outpatient surgery. Sometimes they want someone to drop everything and stand by for several hours *during* the procedure.

If your family lives 2000 miles away and your friends have demanding jobs, your friendly surgical coordinator will sneer, "What's the matter, don't you have any friends?"

When they tried that one on me, I asked: "Could you take time off to pick up a friend in the middle of the day?" She replied, without seeing the irony, "Of course not! I have to work."

Posting on social media and in newspaper comment sections, people tell stories of foregoing medical procedures when they can't get a ride home. They hire Uber drivers and strangers from Craigslist who will pretend to be friends. They sneak out the back door when nobody's looking.

The hospital's answer? "It's not our problem."

(2) Simply being alone tends to be defined as "lonely."

Years ago, when I was living in New York City, I encountered a thirty-something woman who lived alone.

"I hate eating alone," she said. 'I feel like I'm the only person in the city who's eating dinner alone."

Really? In New York City? Eight million people and nobody's eating alone?

It's a quick jump from "I'm alone" to, "I must be lonely!"

In his otherwise excellent book, *Modern Death*, Haider Warraich writes about a woman who "came in [to the hospital] by herself." She didn't have a health care proxy and didn't have anyone who would know her preferences.

Warraich then points out that by 2030, this woman's situation won't be unusual. By then 2 million Americans will have outlived all their family and friends. He also notes that social networks have changed, with people reporting far fewer confidants.

So far so good. But then Warraich goes on to assume this woman is lonely.

He writes: "The next day, in a lovely gesture, my attending physician brought a bouquet of fall flowers and a copy of the New York Times for my *lonesome* patient. Perhaps more than the antibiotics we were giving her, it was that gesture which was the most significant intervention that we made for her." [Emphasis added.]

Why does he assume this woman is lonesome? Maybe she's got lots of friends who were just too busy to come to the hospital with her. They probably couldn't get time off from work.

The woman's reaction might not be about loneliness at all. The idea of a medical professional doing something nice would blow me away -- not because I'd be relieved of loneliness, but because they showed respect for my dignity and intelligence. Usually, they treat me like a sack of potatoes ("We're not ready for you: wait over there.") or a five-year-old ("Sit up nice and tall for me.").

What would be an even greater concern is her lack of a health care proxy. The truth is, it's not easy to find the people your estates and trusts lawyer wants you to have.

Besides, it shouldn't be necessary. The whole concept is outdated, based on the 1950s idea that people in your life were available to arrive at your bedside at a moment's notice. You should be able to leave instructions on a password-protected online site, so you just provide access when you check into a hospital. Your medical proxy could be vacationing in Bali when the time comes, even if they're family members.

(3) When you're somewhere north of fifty, you're expected to make friends with people "your own age."

When you're 35, do you have a lot in common with other people just because they're also 35?

Even in high school, you probably didn't love everyone your own age. If you were a party-going sports fan you probably didn't mingle with classmates who listed "reading" as a hobby and thought the Dallas Cowboys were a country music band.

In your sixties and seventies, you're even less likely to share common interests and values with people "your own age" than you were in high school. In her book *Out of Time*, Lynne Segal makes this point: people tend to become "more rather than less different from each other with the accumulation of time," especially with regard to issues of death and old age.

But it's awfully convenient to insist that older people befriend one another, especially for anyone who wants to hide older people away in a ghetto, cleverly disguised as a "senior living community."

(4) To relieve loneliness, we're supposed to talk to strangers

In her book *Women Rowing North*, Mary Pipher suggests striking up conversations with people of all ages. Noting the work ethic of a grocery bagger, she suggests we say, "Who taught you to work like that?"

In my experience, the young man would see you as a new parent figure and shrug you off with, "Dunno.".

I love talking to strangers myself. I always have. I'm curious about other people's lives, especially their careers. My friends tease me about my propensity to ask probing questions as if I were an investigative journalist or a private detective.

During my twenties, I took jobs that kept me on the road - traveling nonstop. Back then flying was much more civilized. I quizzed the airline staff about their work schedules and their training. I quizzed people who sat next to me on airplanes, as long as they seemed sane and didn't put a priority on saving my soul.

When I got my Covid shot, many years later, I quizzed the sailors and Marines at the Philadelphia Convention Center. What was their status? Did they get to stay in nice hotels? How did they like Philly?

But I don't talk to my real friends that way. Conversations with strangers don't compensate for an absence of meaningful connection.

The idea that "being with anybody is better than being alone" will lead to some pretty awful situations. Christiane Northrup, author of *Goddesses Never Age*, says,

"Your ageless years are also a time for making new friends with youthful energy who don't dwell on the past or talk about illnesses and doctors...If you want to remain ageless, you need to create a subculture of individuals who are living healthfully and joyfully."

I'll drink to that...but why stereotype this kind of energy as "youthful?" We all know thirty-somethings whose negative energy leaves us feeling drained.

Then there's Joan Rivers, Winston Churchill, Queen Elizabeth II, Pablo Picasso, Olga Kotelko, Gloria Steinem, Martha Stewart, and Willie Murphy ...all examples of high energy at age 80 and beyond.

(5) We're supposed to make friends in age-appropriate places.

When you read any articles on loneliness, you'll always see comments like, "People who complain that they are lonely need to find themselves a hobby, join a church, or volunteer their time for a good cause."

That's the holy trinity of recommendations for older people and they're consistent with the Miss Congeniality role assigned to us. They're also consistent with beliefs about the working life of people over a certain age.

Want more friends? Do something hard.

Those chirpy articles never mention one of the most important facts. People often make friends when they meet a challenge together.

In *What Makes Olga Run*, Bruce Grierson points to the special bond that existed among competitors of all ages. These bonds, he noted, come from the shared backgrounds of training in a tough sport.

People in the military, starting with military academies, form tight bonds because they've shared extremely challenging experiences. People who work on challenging projects on a job will form bonds that hold long after some have moved on.

Shared purpose lets you get past age differences and bond with others based on what you care about. Several news stories featured a sixty-three-year-old sophomore at Reinhardt College. She studies for exams, writes papers, worries about grades ...and plays on the golf team. She's not the team mom: she's a teammate.

I've been a member of IndyHall, a coworking space in Philadelphia, since 2011. While they were temporarily running virtually as I write this paragraph, I joined RecPhilly, identified as a space for "creatives."

In both those places, I connect with people who are less than half my age. We talk about the best equipment for a podcast, the cheapest way to store files in the cloud, and the best place nearby to get a decent lunch. They never ask me for advice. If you suggested they view me as a sage, they'd text LMAO – laughing their asses off.

You can bond over non-work activities, of course - if you have a strong shared purpose or you bring a shared background. Olga herself built her life around track and field competitions. I've made connections myself through comedy and improv classes. I have energizing conversations with people at the gym. I don't do any of those things to meet people. I just do what I want…pretty much as always.

Loneliness as a Personality Trait

A Next Avenue blog reports a novel argument by Dr. Dilip Jeste, a psychiatrist associated with UC San Diego. Loneliness, Jeste says, can be viewed as a personality trait, which means it can be modified. You might feel lonely because you have just five friends.

Jeste says you can reframe your thoughts in one of two ways. You can say, "Five friends - I can leverage these relationships to make more friends." Or you can say, "Five friends - the perfect number."

What you're doing here is changing the narrative. You can feel empowered by being alone. You can redefine aloneness as solitude, not loneliness.

You can have 12 kids and 100 friends … and still die alone.

One of my favorite Kacey Musgaves songs, Merry-Go-Round, ridicules the tradition that if you don't have two children by the time you're twenty-one, you're doomed to die alone.

Supreme Court Justice Antonin Scalia died alone on a hunting trip, leaving a wife, 9 children, and 56 grandchildren. England's Queen Elizabeth II sat alone in a pew during her husband's funeral. Her children are scattered or disgraced. Like Scalia, she could die alone.

Frankly, dying alone seems infinitely preferable to dying in a hospital with tubes and needles, not to mention a roommate who brings a host of noisy (and nosy) relatives to the scene. It's preferable to family standing around your bed, speculating on who will inherit your worldly goods. And it's definitely not a reason to go out and find a total stranger to accompany you on your final hours in the world.

An Aging Bitch will stop trying to "escape loneliness" and start "embracing solitude."

If you're going to talk about loneliness, you also need to mention the downside of desperately seeking friendship. When someone tries too hard to be a friend, they'll be even more isolated.

Like many writers on aging, Christiane Northrup talks about the need for community. Unlike most of them, she stresses the need to be careful about who we admit into our lives. Cut the "energetic cord," she says, when you meet someone who drains your life force.

It works both ways. I've walked away from people whose energy wasn't helping me. And I've been "ghosted" by people who presumably felt I wasn't helping them. It's nothing personal. Sometimes you just need a different kind of energy in your life.

Without getting all woo-wooey, I've found that giving up a relationship - whether it's my choice or theirs - invariably opens space for new, fulfilling opportunities.

It's back to the bank loans principle. Friends show up when you least need them. Stop being needy and your life will be filled with meaningful relationships.

Chapter 16: "Getting My AB Degree: A Certified Aging Bitch"

"Age is not the enemy. Stagnation is the enemy. Complacency is the enemy. All animate creatures are destroyed when frozen. They do not move. This is not a worthy goal." – Twyla Tharp, choreographer, in her book *Keep It Moving*.

"'Old age,' as we know it, is made up—and this concept is hurting everyone." - Joseph Coughlin, in MIT Technology Review.

An awful lot of people subscribe to the stereotypes. You're expected to associate getting old with getting sick, weak, slow, and dumb. You're expected to tolerate dismissive insults, such as "geezer." You're a consumer, not a producer.

Most of all, you're expected to accept the inevitability of what happens "at your age."

Never again!

In this book, I've argued that it's not about age after all. Something else is going on.

Here are 3 mantras to focus your thoughts about aging in a new way.

Mantra #1: Age isn't chronological: it's cultural.

If I say, "When I was a girl, women played three-on-three basketball," I'm old.

But what if I said, "In my culture, women played three-on-three basketball." Most people would say, "Oh, how interesting!"

We're all shaped by our cultures and by the way we grew up. We're also shaped by the culture and experiences associated with the era of our childhood.

Unconsciously, many of us may already view age as culture.

Writing in *The New York Times*, Emily Labes-Warren noted that how people feel about their own age can predict their health and likelihood of dying. She writes, "Paradoxically, older people may hold warm feelings for their generation even as they feel distaste for people their age."

Yet this feeling doesn't seem paradoxical when you view age as culture. Generations share values, attitudes, and experiences; aging effects often derive from age cohorts, not from age itself. And cohorts create culture.

"We're not that special."

In 1972, over 50 years ago, Aline Duerk made news by becoming the first admiral in the US Navy. Today it's still noteworthy but not a big deal.

In 2019, Lori Lightfoot, a black female lesbian married to a Caucasian woman, became mayor of Chicago. That was newsworthy but growing old fast.

Now the Vice President of the United States is a Black-Asian woman married to a Jewish white man. The Jewish white man has become friends with the husband of a gay male Cabinet member.

We're getting close: I'm waiting for the first black female lesbian *atheist* to become president of the United States. That'll be worth a slot on the six o'clock news.

So why do we still get excited when a ninety-year-old runs a marathon or wins a dance contest? Title IX was passed in 1972. A girl who was 12 at the time would be born around 1960. She'll be 80 in 2040.

On the near horizon is a whole generation of women who grew up thinking it's normal to compete on varsity athletic teams. You can bet a large number of those women will still be running on their ninetieth birthday. It's in the culture. And it's no big deal.

Let's leave "age" off the intake forms.

In her book, *This Chair Rocks*, Ashton Applewhite points out that "reflexively" identifying people by age is nothing but a "bad habit."

After all, we no longer identify people by marital status. Even the stately *New York Times* refers to women as "Ms." rather than forcing them to be identified by marital status as "Miss" or "Mrs."

Why, Applewhite asks, should age be different? "There are plenty of ways to clue readers in, for the rare event that it's actually relevant to the story," she says.

Her best suggestion is to remove the date of birth from medical records.

At first, the idea seems unthinkable. But it might lead to better medical outcomes.

Doctors notoriously define patients in terms of their age. It's not unusual to hear recommendations for screening tests based solely on the numbers. Colonoscopies have become a rite of passage for many fifty-year-olds.

In fact, age irrelevance will be good for people of all ages. A blogger on the Love What Matters blog cited numerous stories of young people who spent years in pain, needlessly. They kept hearing, "You're too young for a chronic disease." Or "you're too young to feel this much pain."

Just google "too young for a gall bladder problem." You'll find at least a dozen heart-felt accounts of misdiagnosed young women.

Mantra #2: "What's good for 'old people' is good for everybody."

Allen Glicksman, Director of Research and Evaluation at the Philadelphia Corporation for Aging, has been widely quoted as saying, "What's good for old people is good for everybody and what's bad for older people is bad for everyone in the community."

Most US cities —and many in other countries - offer senior transportation passes, giving you discounts or free rides on most public transit systems. Medicare makes medical care affordable. Lots of people who dread getting older will nevertheless count the days to their 65th birthdays just to get Medicare.

The truth is, when you run the world for "older people" you'll benefit everyone.

In her book, *This Chair Rocks*, Ashton Applewhite writes about an able-bodied person who bought a home from a wheelchair user.

"Damn," the new homeowner says, "it's nice to have wide doorways -- and the toilet positioned this way. They should just do it for everyone." (p 15).

Exactly. That's what universal design is all about for the built environment: creating spaces that will be enjoyed by all kinds of people. Imagine an airline with economy seats tailored to people who come in economy size. I'll drink to that.

But the principle applies to services as well.

Public transportation.

Older people sometimes can't drive. But more and more younger people don't *want* to drive.

We're spending millions on highways. Car accidents take a huge toll on medical services, law enforcement, and human life. Thousands of people enter prisons every year to serve sentences for DUIs.

If everyone could ride public transit free or cheap, we'd save a fortune, not to mention a lot of lives. We'd spare families the misery of losing their loved ones to death or incarceration.

Senior emergency rooms in hospitals.

Imagine an ER with floors with more traction, gentler lighting, personal rooms for patients, blankets warmed in special ovens, and large-print clocks. Most people would appreciate those features whether they're nineteen or ninety.

Mantra #3: Replace your Inner Old Person with your Inner Aging Bitch

You've probably heard of self-improvement programs urging you to get in touch with your "inner child." Life Coach Nicole Lewis-Keeber talks about paying attention to your "inner kiddo." The framework seems to be based loosely on Freudian id-ego-superego model of the human psyche and on a book written over fifty years ago by Thomas Harris, "I'm OK, You're OK."

The idea is that we're influenced by long-held beliefs when we make decisions. These beliefs go back to our childhood. They're based on what we were told or how we understood the world back then. And of course, because we were children, we didn't always get things right. We didn't know how to apply what we learned.

For instance, suppose you had overprotective parents who freaked out when you tripped and skinned your knee. You might have gotten the message, "The world is a scary place. Being frightened is normal."

When you experience something new, your Inner Child says, "Uh oh, the world is scary" and begins to feel frightened.

I'm willing to bet that we also carry around an Inner Old Person. She's the spirit, the voice, and the belief system we've been taught to associate with "getting older."

You hear her voice when you catch yourself saying, "I'm getting too old to do this." Or, "What can you expect from someone my age?"

Or she warns you not to wear shorts after your forty-first birthday: what will people think?

Or she's whispering that you should expect to slow down when you're fifty and get back pain when you're sixty.

She judges other "older" people too.

"Doesn't she realize that dress is too young for her?"

"Why doesn't she date someone her own age?"

"That woman in the gym must be at least eighty - she's amazing."

If you keep hearing warnings about the consequences of aging, it's your Inner Old Person speaking: the voice you've been taught to accept. The problem isn't that she's old; the problem is that she's infiltrated your mind with every stereotype on the planet. And you have to resist.

Create a dialogue.

My Inner Old Person shows up when I've got a work assignment I'm not particularly excited about. She sighs, "You shouldn't have to work this hard at your age. You should be relaxing on a beach somewhere."

If I'm lucky, my Inner Bitch responds, "Ridiculous! Nancy Pelosi is older than I am. Herding cats in Congress is a lot harder than anything I'm doing."

"Anyway," my Inner Bitch continues, "you've never liked beaches. You *like* to work. And you could use the money. You like flying first class, remember? Shut up and deal!"

Talk to your Inner Old Person. Ask where she got those ideas. Show some tough love. Be her coach.

When your Inner Old Person mutters, "You can't do that at your age," your Inner Aging Bitch needs to say, "Shut the fuck up."

Mantra #4: Go out with a bang and a celebration.

A few years ago, I was attending a talk on business planning. The leader said, "Now I want you all to imagine yourself ten years from now."

A fellow attendee, who's a few years younger than I am, turned to me with a horrified look on her face.

"I hope I'm still here," she said.

At a certain point, the question, "What do you want people to write on your tombstone?" becomes a serious question – not a light-hearted career change exercise.

For me, it was the realization that, "My winter coat may live longer than I do."

It was making provisions in my will for the cats, who most likely will outlive me, who should not end up in a shelter, meowing inconsolably at the volunteers.

And it was hoping the pandemic would end in time to cross off two more trips on my bucket list.

Don't go gentle.

All too often, children think they're being kind when they urge their parents to "take it easy."

Remember the BBC's re-creation of Ellen Langer's aging experiment? One staff member felt horrible as she watched an 80-something woman struggling to get her luggage up the stairs. That woman walked away easily after two weeks.

So next Christmas, forget about giving your aging relatives a comforter and a six-pack of chamomile tea. Give them three sessions with the toughest personal trainer you can find. They may dis-invite you from the family's holiday dinner but sometime in the next year, they'll thank you.

You don't grow unless you push yourself.

I must admit, it's not always easy.

When I started doing standup comedy, I didn't know enough to be scared. Now, even when I'm confident of my material and my timing, I'm nervous every single time. Will I forget what I'm supposed to say? Will I stumble? Will I drop the microphone?

One of my scariest experiences of 2021 was going to Small Claims Court, protesting a "miscellaneous fee" my condo added to the seller documents when I moved out. On the way to the hearing, I kept thinking, "Why on earth am I doing this? I should have listened to the friend who told me to forget it."

When I work out at the gym, or when I go for a long walk, I'm often tempted to say, "Let's forget this and go get some coffee ice cream."

When I have to learn new software (which is like learning to operate a toaster over and over again) or do something tedious (like organize this book for publishing), I'm tempted to find a porch and a rocking chair.

That's my Inner Old Person speaking.

Pushing beyond your comfort zone is the only way to grow. You don't have to do anything crazy. You can study a tough academic subject online. You can work in a competitive field. Or you can emulate Olga Kotelko and take up track and field, if you've got the knees for it.

My friends have other ways to describe the way I'm living my life. The term "drama queen" has been mentioned. I embrace that identity. Nobody feels sorry for a drama queen.

Seeing the end in sight can mean freedom.

I've heard people say that approaching death feels like coming home.

I can relate...sort of. I don't have a sense of a home waiting for me. I feel more like I'm getting ready for a major move or a long vacation.

There are a lot of things left to do.

But there's also a sense of freedom. It's okay to bend the rules and eat the foods I really like, at least most of the time. Doctors tell me there isn't much that can affect my all-cause mortality. I can start smoking again if I want to (and I would, except there's no place to smoke anymore, and I want to keep doing Zumba).

Food? My rule is, "If you buy it at the farmer's market, it's healthy, and you can eat as much as you want."

It's okay to take a day off to do nothing. It's okay to upgrade to first class because...well, just because.

Getting ready for the Final Exit.

When you're getting ready for a trip, there's no point in filling up the fridge before you go. And for some things, the return on investment just isn't there. "Delayed gratification" leads to the question of, "Delayed till when?"

Before a vacation, you leave a list for the people who take care of your house and your pets. I've started making lists of things I want people to take care of when I'm gone. I made a will, with provisions for someone who will make sure the cats never, ever end up in a shelter...and a backup in case that person's not around.

I'm also writing instructions for my memorial service...a list of songs to play or sing while everyone drinks beer and eats pizza.

They'll tell stories about all the dumb and crazy things they saw me do. Hopefully they'll shed a tear or two...because they're laughing so hard.

And they'll say, "She did some good. She was funny. And yes... [little wince here] she could be a bitch.

"Thank goodness."

Aging Broad Manifesto

I hope this book has given you a new perspective on growing older. If you've felt a spark of anger as you read some of the sections, I've accomplished my goal. If you've laughed out loud at some other sections, I'm even more pleased.

My hope is that, after reading this book, you'll feel empowered to speak out against stereotypes. You won't worry about hurting someone's feelings when you remind them they're insensitive to yours. You might even decide to use some strong language to make your point.

If you're still some distance away from the aging zone, hopefully you'll be inspired to make realistic but tough plans. You'll make economic choices that leave you in control of your life. You'll start working out right away to build muscle, stay flexible and raise your body awareness. You'll refuse to accept illness, poverty, or isolation as an inevitable part of aging.

Most of all, I hope you'll feel motivated to speak out for change.

If you're in a country where you can write to your legislators, write to all of them and make your feelings known. Loudly and often, please.

Tell them you don't want to spend your last years as a helpless person with no quality of life. You want the option to check out when you're ready, without a lot of red tape and hassle.

Tell them to offer everyone a tattoo or bracelet with a link to their final wishes, with no need for a human proxy to be on the scene. You shouldn't have to suffer if your proxy happens to be vacationing in Fiji in a cell-phone-free zone. There's no reason why we can't decide in advance how we want to die, even if we get dementia.

Or if you're worried the opposite way, tell them you want access to medical treatment as long as you can breathe, instead of being dismissed as "too old."

Speak out to your medical and mental health providers. Refuse to tolerate a condescending conversation. Refuse a diagnosis of "because you're old."

Refuse to accept treatment, tests, or prescriptions without question. When you're treated with incompetence or rudeness, take the time to write an intelligent letter to the provider and/or the facility. Sometimes you'll be dismissed but other times you'll be surprised to receive a respectful reply.

Don't let people scam you out of your money because they think, "She won't bother fighting this." Add the Attorney General's contact info to your address book.

Remind the Attorney General the office is elective and you vote.

Write reviews of books about aging.

Applaud the good ones. Tear apart the ones that hold out false hope or reinforce the stereotypes. (You can do this literally. Use the pages to line your cat's litter box.)

Don't be afraid to be vicious. A former friend distanced himself after he saw my scathing review of one of those chirpy-cheery "getting a job after 50" books. His loss.

Never, ever let people call you a codger or a geezer or some other insulting name. Never accept those designations for yourself. They're not funny. Ridicule is the first stop on the path to abuse.

Never let anyone tell you to dress or act appropriately "for your age." Too old for shorts? Not supposed to eat certain foods after fifty? Practice saying, "Do I look like I give a fuck?"

Never accept any advice or criticism that begins, "At your age…"

When they call you a bitch, smile and say, "Thank you. I live for this."

If you'd like to get in touch, please visit my websites:

AgingInSneakers.com (my irreverent blog on aging)

CathyGoodwin.com (marketing and online copywriting)

MidlifeCareerStrategy.com (career change for midlife, mid-career professionals)

Don't forget to write a review of this book. You'll help get the message out to others who will benefit.

ACKNOWLEDGMENTS AND DEDICATION

Thanks to the friends who read advance versions of this book and made suggestions, especially my Indy Hall coworkers Alex Hillman, Pam Selle and Adam Teterus; Eskadar Getahun from the Barnard Book Club; and Scarlet Estelle from RecPhily. Thanks to Michele PW and her publishing company for helping me with the logistics that seemed overwhelming.

This book is dedicated to my Philadelphia coworking spaces – IndyHall and RecPhilly. When I go there, I feel ageless. All anybody cares about is, "Can you do tech? Are you a creator? Do you have a podcast?" and most important, "Where's a decent place to get lunch around here?" They would ROFL if you suggested I filled the role of an aging sage.

PLEASE VISIT MY WEBSITE – AgingInSneakers.com
You'll find new articles, resources, updates, links and more.

DO YOU NEED A SPEAKER?
I'm available to speak to groups remotely or in person. I'm delighted to be interviewed or do a guest gig for your podcast or blog. Reach out to me at http://CathyGoodwin.com/contact

References

INTRODUCTION

"Gloria Steinem on being called a bitch" – YouTube Video
https://youtu.be/5gYXQ6PUjR4

Aronson, Louise (2019), Elderhood: Redefining Aging, Transforming Medicine, Reimagining Life, Bloomsbury Publishing.

Painter, Nell Irvin (2018), Old in Art School: A Memoir of Starting Over, Counterpoint

Pipher, Mary (2019) The Joy of Being a Woman in her 70s, New York Times, Jan 12

Ericsson,Anders, and Robert Pool, (2016) Peak: Secrets from the New Science of Expertise, Harper One

Grierson, Bruce (2014), What If Age Were Nothing But a Mindset? New York Times, Oct 22

Segal, Lynne, (2013) *Out of Time: The Pleasures and Perils of Aging*, Verso.

Barnes, Julian (1986), *Staring at the Sun*, Generic.

Chapter 1

Langer, Ellen and Mihnea Moldoveanu, (2000), Mindfulness Research and the Future, *Journal of Social Issues*, Vol 56 , No 1, 129-139.

Applewhite, Ashton (2021), Let's Climb Out Of the Generation Trap," Next Avenue blog, June 29. Retrieved from https://www.nextavenue.org/generation-trap/

Swardson, Nick (2022), quoted in online page, Jokes4Us. Retrieved from http://www.jokes4us.com/peoplejokes/comedianjokes/nickswardsonjokes.html

Richardson, Ann (2021), Is Age Just a Number? Do you feel hesitant to reveal your age?"

Nov 12 Retrieved from https://sixtyandme.com/is-age-just-a-number-do-you-feel-hesitant-to-reveal-your-age/

"franmarta," (2013) "Short-Timer Syndrome   Urban Dictionary, Mar 12. Retrieved from https://www.urbandictionary.com/define.php?term=short%20timer%20syndrome

Grierson, Bruce, (2014) *What Makes Olga Run?: The Mystery of the 90-Something Track Star and What She Can Teach Us About Living Longer, Happier Lives*. Henry Holt & Co.

Emanuel Ezekiel J. (2014) Why I Hope To Die At 75. The Atlantic, October.
https://www.theatlantic.com/magazine/archive/2014/10/why-i-hope-to-die-at-75/379329/

Dweck, Carol, (2006), Mindset: The New Psychology of Success. Random House.

Rufo, Christopher (director), (2012) Age of Champions movie, New Video studio

Chapter 2

"Joan Rivers on Graham Norton," Uploaded by "Chris F," YouTube Video. https://youtu.be/4DbPFupvkRk [date not found]

Musgraves, Kacey (2015) "Pageant Material," Studio Album by Mercury Nashville. Retrieved from YouTube
https://youtu.be/sEVX_FrgGWU

Anonymous, Readers Digest jokes, retrieved from
https://www.rd.com/jokes/#the-problem-with-jury-duty-joke/

Fleck, Alissa (2018), Why Postmates Agreed to Retract Its Tasteless Ad About Age, and Death. Adweek onlie edition May 23.

Retrieved from
https://www.adweek.com/brand-marketing/why-postmates-agreed-to-retract-its-tasteless-ad-about-age-and-death/

Brown, Brene, (2007) (but it isn't): Making the Journey from "What Will People Think?" to "I Am Enough" – Avery.

Funny Prayer About Getting Old, Uploaded by Home Instead, Retrieved at
https://youtu.be/vPFCn3itBFE

Mallon, Thomas (1998) "Space Aged," New York Times, June 14.

Hilt, Michael L. (2000), "Descriptive Analysis of News Magazines' Coverage of John Glenn's Return to Space" Communication Faculty Publications. 60.
https://digitalcommons.unomaha.edu/commfacpub/60

Wojciechowski, Michele (2021), "Stupid Things Not To Do When You Get Older," Next Avenue, August 30.

https://www.nextavenue.org/steven-petrow-stupid-things/

Levy BR, Pilver CE, Pietrzak RH. (2014) Lower prevalence of psychiatric conditions when negative age stereotypes are resisted. Soc Sci Med. Oct;119:170-4. doi: 10.1016/j.socscimed.2014.06.046. Epub 2014 Jul 3. PMID: 25189737; PMCID: PMC4372137.

Span Paula (2019), Ageism: A 'Prevalent and Insidious' Health Threat, New York Times, April 26.

Grierson, Bruce (2014), What Makes Olga Run?: The Mystery of the 90-Something Track Star and What She Can Teach Us About Living Longer, Happier Lives. Henry Holt and Co

Uploaded by TEDX TALKS 12

What if age is just a state of mind? | Bruce Grierson | TEDxPSU YouTube Video

Retrieved from
https://youtu.be/56JMahuMlvE

Chapter 3

Dampier, Cindy (2014) Talking to the elderly shouldn't include baby talk — it's not only condescending, it can cause cognitive harm. Chicago Tribune, Oct 4.

Leland, John (2008), In *'Sweetie' and 'Dear,' a Hurt for the Elderly*, New York Times, Oct 6

Wikipedia Article, *Elderspeak*. Last revised Mar 13 2022
https://en.wikipedia.org/wiki/Elderspeak

Hooper, Susan (2017), *Please Don't Call Me "Hon"* Psych Central May 29.

https://www.psychologytoday.com/us/blog/detours-and-tangents/201705/please-don-t-call-me-hon

Leland, John (2008), In 'Sweetie' and 'Dear,' a Hurt for the Elderly, New York Times, Oct 6

Chapter 4

Quotes Investigator (2018) –undated - The Greatest Trick the Devil Ever Pulled Was Convincing the World He Didn't Exist

Retrieved from
https://quoteinvestigator.com/2018/03/20/devil/

Originally: YouTube video, Title: The greatest trick the devil ever pulled was to convince the world he didn't exist, Uploaded on April 30, 2009, Uploaded by: iPhilR, (Quotation starts at 0 minute 4 seconds of 3 minutes 2 seconds) (Video excerpt from the 1995 movie "The Usual Suspects" Phrase spoken by Kevin Spacey as Verbal)

Span, Paula (2022), Exploring the Health Effects of Aging, New York Times, April 23. Retrieved from
https://www.nytimes.com/2022/04/23/health/ageism-levy-elderly.html#commentsContainer

Northrup, Christiane (2016), *Goddesses Never Age: The Secret Prescription for Radiance, Vitality, and Well-Being*. Hay House.

Black, Virginia (2016) He's 75 and gets carded at Kroger. It's irritating, not flattering South Bend Tribune, Feb 1.

Jean Becker [director] 2010 My afternoons with Marguerite, movie. StudioCanal.

Banas, Andrew (2019)," 'He picked the wrong house': Bodybuilder, 82, fights break-in suspect" WHAM Channel 13 ABC. Retrieved from https://13wham.com/news/local/he-picked-the-wrong-house-82-year-old-beats-up-break-in-suspect

Nortin M Hadler (2019), Rethinking Aging: Growing Old and Living Well in an Overtreated Society. University of North Carolina Press.

Albright, Madeleine (2012), Prague Winter: A Personal Story of Remembrance and War, 1937-1948 Kindle Edition. Harper.

Bursack, Carol Bradley (2022), How to Convince Your Parent to Move to Assisted Living. Aging Care Blog Mar 22. Retrieved from https://www.agingcare.com/articles/convincing-parent-assisted-living-142136.htm

Collins, Gail, No Stopping Us Now:The Adventures of Older Women in American History (2019), Little Brown and Company.

Bloomberg News (2015), [Video] Japan's Elderly Inmates Pick Prison Over Freedom, April 16. Retrieved from https://www.bloomberg.com/news/videos/2015-04-16/why-some-of-japan-s-elderly-want-to-go-to-jail

Lachs, Mark (2011), *What Your Doctor Won't Tell You About Getting Older: An Insider's Survival Manual for Outsmarting the Health-Care System*. Penguin Books.

Fukada, Shiho (2018) Japan's Prisons Are a Haven for Elderly Women, Mar 16
https://www.bloomberg.com/news/features/2018-03-16/japan-s-prisons-are-a-haven-for-elderly-women

Span, Paula (2016) Loneliness Can Be Deadly for Elders; Friends Are the Antidote. The New York Times, Dec 30
https://www.nytimes.com/2016/12/30/health/loneliness-elderly.html

Leland, John (2018): *Happiness Is a Choice You Make: Lessons from a Year Among the Oldest Old*. Sarah Crichton Books.

Nursing Home Abuse Guide (n.d.), Retrieved from
https://www.nursinghomeabuseguide.org/nursing-home-abuse-statistics/

Castle, Nicholas (2012), Nurse Aides' Reports of Resident Abuse in Nursing Homes. *Journal of Applied Gerontology*. Vol. 31, Issue #3.

Hawes, Catherine (2003), Elder Abuse in Residential Long-Term Care Settings: What Is Known and What Information Is Needed?

Chapter 14 in National Research Council (US) Panel to Review Risk and Prevalence of Elder Abuse and Neglect; Bonnie RJ, Wallace RB, editors. Washington (DC): National Academies Press (US).

Aging in Sneakers Website: References for Nursing Home Abuse
https://aginginsneakers.com/references-nursing-home-abuse/

Website, The Greenhouse Project.
https://thegreenhouseproject.org/

Semuels, Alana (2015), Building Better Nursing Homes, Atlantic Monthly, April 21. Retrieved from
https://www.theatlantic.com/business/archive/2015/04/a-better-nursing-home-exists/390936/

Cunningham-Cook, Matthew (2021), Nursing Home Industry Avoids Scrutiny For Covid-19 Deaths as Powerful Lobby Goes To Work. The Intercept. February 20. Retrieved from
https://theintercept.com/2021/02/20/covid-nursing-home-cuomo-clyburn/

Jaffe, Ina (2020), For-Profit Nursing Homes' Pleas For Government Money Brings Scrutiny. NPR.org (October 22). Retrieved from
https://www.npr.org/2020/10/22/918432908/for-profit-nursing-homes-pleas-for-government-money-brings-scrutiny

Chapter 6

Extence, Gavin, (2014) The Universe Versus Alex Woods,

Redhook Reprint Edition.

Jacoby, Susan (2011), *Never Say Die: The Myth and Marketing of the New Old Age, Vintage.*

Brody, Jane E. (2007), A Common Casualty of Old Age:The Will To Live. New York Times. Nov 27.
https://www.nytimes.com/2007/11/27/health/27brod.html

Coughlin, Joseph F. (2017) The Longevity Economy: Unlocking the World's Fastest-Growing, Most Misunderstood Market. PublicAffairs.

Applewhite, Ashton (2019) , *This Chair Rocks: A Manifesto Against Ageism,*

Butler, Katy (2013), *Knocking on Heaven's Door: The Path to a Better Way of Death*, Scribner.

Boudreau, Evan (2017), Hospice to Provide Safe Haven From Euthanasia for Patients and Doctors, National Catholic Register, March 14. Retrieved from
https://www.catholicregister.org/item/24677-hospice-to-provide-safe-haven-from-euthanasia-for-patients-and-doctors

Gurian, Michael (2013), *The Wonder of Aging: A New Approach to Embracing Life After Fifty* (Atria Books, reprint edition)

Grierson, Bruce, (2014) *What Makes Olga Run?: The Mystery of the 90-Something Track Star and What She Can Teach Us About Living Longer, Happier Lives*. Henry Holt & Co.

Bever, Lindsey (2018) This Australian scientist just turned 104. Now he's flying to Switzerland to die. Washington Post. May 3.

Chapter 7

Jacoby, Susan (2011), Never Say Die: *The Myth and Marketing of the New Old Age*, Vintage.

The Intern, Movie.

Conley, Chris (2018). *Wisdom at Work: The Making of a Modern Elder.* Currency.

Schachter-Shalomi (2008), From Age-ing to Sage-ing: *A Revolutionary Approach to Growing Older*. Grand Central Publishing.

Leland, John (2018): *Happiness Is a Choice You Make: Lessons from a Year Among the Oldest Old*. Sarah Crichton Books.

Chapter 8

Stevens, Heidi (2017), Jane Fonda's frank sex toy talk opens the door for a generation. Chicago Tribune, May 2. Retrieved from https://www.chicagotribune.com/columns/heidi-stevens/ct-jane-fonda-vibrator-ellen-balancing-0502-20170502-column.html

Marine, Brooke (2019), Jane Fonda Opens Up About Comedy and Mental Health, May 29. Retrieved from https://www.wmagazine.com/story/jane-fonda-grace-and-frankie-mental-health-interview

Renkl, Margaret (2018), The Gift of Menopause, New York Times, Augusg 5. Retrieved from https://www.nytimes.com/2018/08/05/opinion/the-gift-of-menopause.html

Nunez, Sigrid (2020), *What Are You Going Through*, Riverhead Books.

Krystal, Arthur (2019), Why We Can't Tell The Truth About Aging, New Yorker. October 28. Retrieved from https://www.newyorker.com/magazine/2019/11/04/why-we-cant-tell-the-truth-about-aging

Northrup, Christiane (2016), *Goddesses Never Age: The Secret Prescription for Radiance, Vitality, and Well-Being*. Hay House.

Stevens, Heidi (2017), Jane Fonda's frank sex toy talk opens the door for a generation. Chicago Tribune, May 2. Retrieved from https://www.chicagotribune.com/columns/heidi-stevens/ct-jane-fonda-vibrator-ellen-balancing-0502-20170502-column.html

Chapter 9

Brody, Jane E. (2007), A Common Casualty of Old Age:The Will To Live. New York Times. Nov 27.
https://www.nytimes.com/2007/11/27/health/27brod.html

Oaklander, Mandi (2016), Old People Are Happier Than People In Their 20s,Time Magazine Aug 24. Retrieved from
https://time.com/4464811/aging-happiness-stress-anxiety-depression/

Leland, John (2017), Want to be happy? Think like an old person. New York Times, December 29, retrieved from
https://www.nytimes.com/2017/12/29/nyregion/want-to-be-happy-think-like-an-old-person.html

Bruce, Debra Fulghum (2020), Depression in Older People, June 4. WebMD Website.
https://www.webmd.com/depression/guide/depression-elderly#1

CDC (page last reviewed Jan 6 2021), Depression is Not a Normal Part of Growing Older. Retrieved from US Center for Disease Control Website
Depression is Not a Normal Part of Growing Older.
https://www.cdc.gov/aging/depression/index.html

Hyman, Mark, MD (2011), Why Anti-Depressants Don't Work for Treating Depression. Huffington Post Blog.

https://www.huffpost.com/entry/depression-medication-why_b_550098

Abrams, Lindsay (2013), Atlantic Monthly, Most People Diagnosed With Depression Do Not Actually Meet Criteria, May 1. Retrieved from
https://www.theatlantic.com/health/archive/2013/05/study-most-people-diagnosed-with-depression-do-not-actually-meet-criteria/275436/

Caplan, Paula J. (1996), They Say You're Crazy: How The World's Most Powerful Psychiatrists Decide Who's Normal. De Capo Lifelong Books.

Hatch, Steven (2016) Snowball in a Blizzard: A Physician's Notes on Uncertainty in Medicine. Basic Books.

Anonymous. 2012. Aging and Depression. APA website. Retrieved from
https://www.apa.org/topics/aging-end-life/depression

Older People, June 4. WebMD Website.
https://www.webmd.com/depression/guide/depression-elderly#1

Brody, Jane E. (2007), A Common Casualty of Old Age:The Will To Live. New York Times. Nov 27.
https://www.nytimes.com/2007/11/27/health/27brod.html

Hari, Johann (2018) Lost Connections: Uncovering the Real Causes of Depression – and the Unexpected Solutions. Bloomsbury USA.

Jacoby, Susan (2011), *Never Say Die: The Myth and Marketing of the New Old Age*, Vintage.

Chapter 10

Williams, Tennessee and Edward Albee (2004), Cat on a Hot Tin Roof, New Directions Press.

Adamczyk, Alicia (2017), Money Magazine website, 5 Inspirational Quotes About Money From Joan Rivers and Other Famous Women, April 21. Retrieved from
https://money.com/quotes-women-money/#:~:text=Joan%20 Rivers%20was%20never%20one,made%2C%22%20she%20 famously%20said.

Ryan, Liz (2014), The Ugly Truth About Age, Discrimination, Forbes Jan 31.
https://www.forbes.com/sites/lizryan/2014/01/31/the-ugly-truth-about-age-discrimination/?sh=45c2bf3c44e7

Hannon, Kerry (2015) Getting the Job You Want After 50 For Dummies. For Dummies, 1st ed.

White, Elizabeth (2019) 55, Underemployed, and Faking Normal: Your Guide to a Better Life. Simon & Schuster.

Collins, Gail, No Stopping Us Now:The Adventures of Older Women in American History (2019), Little Brown and Company.

Chapter 11

Tvedten, Brother Benet (2000), The View From A Monastery. Riverhead Books.

Farrell, Chris (2014) Unretirement: How Baby Boomers are Changing the Way We Think About Work, Community, and the Good Life. Bloomsbury Press.

Chittister, Sister Joan (2008). The Gift of Years. Darton, Longman & Todd Ltd

Wu C, Odden MC, Fisher GG, Stawski RS. (2015) Association of retirement age with mortality: a population-based longitudinal study among older adults in the USA. J Epidemiol Community Health. 2016 Sep;70(9):917-23. doi: 10.1136/jech-2015-207097. Epub 2016 Mar 21. PMID: 27001669; PMCID: PMC6524971.

Chamberlin, Jamie (2014), "Retiring Minds Want To Know," American Psychological Association. Retrieved from https://www.apa.org/monitor/2014/01/retiring-minds

Brown, Melissa, et al., (2010) Working in Retirement, A 21st Century Pnenomenon, Families and Work Institute. Retrieved from https://www.familiesandwork.org/research/2010/working-in-retirement-a-21st-century-phenomenon

Guillebeau, Chris (n.d.), Internal Adventures: On the Road With Betsy and Warren Talbot. Blog post retrieved from https://archive.chrisguillebeau.com/on-the-road-with-betsy-and-warren-talbot/

Chapter 12

Chapman, Stephen (2011), New Bill Gates interview: "Legacy is a stupid thing! I don't want a legacy." Posted in Between the Lines blog on June 12. Retrieved from https://www.zdnet.com/article/new-bill-gates-interview-legacy-is-a-stupid-thing-i-dont-want-a-legacy/

Crittenden, Jennifer and Butler, Sandy (2020), "Juggling Multiple Roles: An Examination of Role Conflict Phase II: RSVP Program Survey Report" *Maine Center on Aging Research and Evaluation*. 39. https://digitalcommons.library.umaine.edu/moca_research/39

TANG, F., MORROW-HOWELL, N., & CHOI, E. (2010). Why do older adult volunteers stop volunteering? Ageing and Society, 30(5), 859-878. doi:10.1017/S0144686X10000140

Landry, Roger (2016), "Should We Stop Being Nice To Older Adults?" Huffington Post. Retrieved from https://www.huffingtonpost.com/roger-landry-md-mph/should-we-stop-being-nice_1_b_7557150.html

Freedman, Marc (2018) How to Live Forever: The Enduring Power of Connecting the Generations. BasicBooks.

Chapter 13

Moynihan R, Doust J, Henry D. Preventing overdiagnosis: how to stop harming the healthy *BMJ* 2012; 344 :e3502 doi:10.1136/bmj.e3502

Spiegel, Alix (2011) How A Bone Disease Grew To Fit the Prescription. NPR. Originally broadcast on All Things Considered. Retrieved from https://www.npr.org/2009/12/21/121609815/how-a-bone-disease-grew-to-fit-the-prescription

Editorial Board of the Wall Street Journal (2020), "The Covid Age Penalty." June 12.

Retrieved from https://www.wsj.com/articles/the-covid-age-penalty-11592003287

Nursing Home Abuse Centers (n.d.), MRSA and Nursing Home Residents. Web page. Last modified Dec 23, 2021. Retrieved from https://www.nursinghomeabusecenter.com/nursing-home-neglect/mrsa/

Luhnow, David and Jose de Cordoba, (2020),

As Covid-19 Hits Developing Countries, Its Victims Are Younger, Wall Street Journal June 19.

Retrieved from https://www.wsj.com/articles/as-covid-19-hits-developing-countries-its-victims-are-younger-11592578205

NBER (2020), What If Virus Lockdowns Targeted People Based on Vulnerability?

National Bureau of Economic Research. The Digest June 6. Retrieved from https://www.nber.org/digest/jun20/what-if-virus-lockdowns-targeted-people-based-vulnerability

Pecci, Alexandra Wilson (2015), 1 IN 5 ADULTS REPORT AGE DISCRIMINATION IN HEALTHCARE SETTINGS, HEALTH LEADERS WEBSITE APRIL 10. RETRIEVED FROM HTTPS://WWW.HEALTHLEADERSMEDIA.COM/CLINICAL-CARE/1-5-ADULTS-REPORT-AGE-DISCRIMINATION-HEALTHCARE-SETTINGS

Lachs, Mark (2011), What Your Doctor Won't Tell You About Getting Older: An Insider's Survival Manual for Outsmarting the Health-Care System. Penguin Books.

Aronson, Louise (2019), Elderhood: Redefining Aging, Transforming Medicine, Reimagining Life, Bloomsbury Publishing.

Healthcare Leadership Council (n.d.), More Physicians No Longer Seeing Medicare Patients. HLC Newsletter. Retrieved from https://www.hlc.org/news/more-physicians-no-longer-seeing-medicare-patients/

Schultz, Josh (2020), Will My Doctor Accept My Medicare Plan? Medicare Resources Website. Retrired from https://www.medicareresources.org/faqs/will-all-doctors-accept-my-medicare-coverage/

Spiegel, Alix (2019) The Tell-Tale Wombs of Lewiston, Maine. National Public Radio. Retrieved from https://www.npr.org/templates/story/story.php?storyId=113571111

Mauney, Matt (2022), Medicare and Observation Services. Retire. com website. Retrieved from https://www.retireguide.com/medicare/services/observation-services/

Emanuel Ezekiel J. (2014) Why I Hope To Die At 75. The Atlantic, October. https://www.theatlantic.com/magazine/archive/2014/10/why-i-hope-to-die-at-75/379329/

Spiegel, Alix (2011) How A Bone Disease Grew To Fit the Prescription. NPR. Originally broadcast on All Things Considered. Retrieved from https://www.npr.org/2009/12/21/121609815/how-a-bone-disease-grew-to-fit-the-prescription

Gaesser, Glenn A. and Siddhartha S. Angadi (2021) Obesity Treatment: Weight Loss Vs. Increasing Fitness and Physical Activity For Health Risks. iScience.September 20.
DOI: https://doi.org/10.1016/j.isci.2021.102995

Chapter 14

Haden, Jeff (n.d.) Science Reveals the Best Age to Start a Thriving Business (It's Much Older Than You Might Think). Inc. Magazine online.
https://www.inc.com/jeff-haden/science-reveals-best-age-to-start-a-thriving-business-is-much-older-than-you-might-think.html

Wojciechowski, Michele (2021), Steven Petrow's Advice On Stupid Things Not to Do When You Get Older. Next Avenue blog, August 30. Retrieved from
https://www.nextavenue.org/steven-petrow-stupid-things/

Krystal, Arthur (2019), Why We Can't Tell The Truth About Aging, New Yorker. October 28. Retrieved from
https://www.newyorker.com/magazine/2019/11/04/why-we-cant-tell-the-truth-about-aging

Emanuel Ezekiel J. (2014) Why I Hope To Die At 75. The Atlantic, October.
https://www.theatlantic.com/magazine/archive/2014/10/why-i-hope-to-die-at-75/379329/

Welch, Gilbert (2016), Less Medicine, More Health: 7 Assumptions That Drive Too Much Medical Care, Beacon Press.

Ben-Harush, A., Shiovitz-Ezra, S., Doron, I., Alon, S., Leibovitz, A., Golander, H., Haron, Y., & Ayalon, L. (2016). Ageism among physicians, nurses, and social workers: findings from a qualitative study. *European journal of ageing*, 14(1), 39–48. https://doi.org/10.1007/s10433-016-0389-9

Northrup, Christiane (2016), *Goddesses Never Age: The Secret Prescription for Radiance, Vitality, and Well-Being*. Hay House.

Aronson, Louise, M.D. (2020) , Age, Complexity, and Crisis — A Prescription for Progress in Pandemic. *New England Journal of Medicine*, July 2, 383:4-6

Niharika Arora Duggal,Ross D. Pollock,Norman R. Lazarus,Stephen Harridge,Janet M. Lord (2018) Major features of immunesenescence, including reduced thymic output, are ameliorated by high levels of physical activity in adulthood. Aging Cell (Vol 17, Issue 2), April.

Stepnowsky, C. J., & Ancoli-Israel, S. (2008). Sleep and Its Disorders in Seniors. *Sleep medicine clinics*, 3(2), 281–293. https://doi.org/10.1016/j.jsmc.2008.01.011

Tanner, R. M., Shimbo, D., Seals, S. R., Reynolds, K., Bowling, C. B., Ogedegbe, G., & Muntner, P. (2016). White-Coat Effect Among Older Adults: Data From the Jackson Heart Study. *Journal of*

clinical hypertension (Greenwich, Conn.), 18(2), 139–145.
https://doi.org/10.1111/jch.12644

Chapter 15

Tillich Paul, n.d quoted in AllGreatQuotes,
https://www.allgreatquotes.com/quote-344538/

Lawrence, Holly (2019), Can Wisdom Protect Against Loneliness?
Next Avenue blog April 11.
https://www.nextavenue.org/can-wisdom-protect-against-loneliness/

Feiler, Bruce (2020), *Life is in the Transitions: Mastering Change At Any Age*, Penguin.

National Academies of Sciences, Engineering, and Medicine. 2020.
Social Isolation and Loneliness in Older Adults: Opportunities for the Health Care System. Washington, DC: The National Academies Press.
https://doi.org/10.17226/25663

Matz-Costa, Christina, (2012) After 55, the Key Is Staying 'Engaged,' Next Avenue Blog March 20.
https://www.nextavenue.org/after-55-key-staying-engaged/

Adamy, Janet (2018) The Loneliest Generation: Americans, More Than Ever, Are Aging Alone

Wall Street Journal, Dec 11.
https://www.wsj.com/articles/the-loneliest-generation-americans-more-than-ever-are-aging-alone-11544541134

King, Marissa (2021) Social Chemistry: Decoding the Patterns of Human Connection. Dutton.

Warraich, Haider (2017), Modern Death: How Medicine Changed the End of Life, St Martin's.

Segal, Lynne, (2013) *Out of Time: The Pleasures and Perils of Aging*, Verso.

Pipher, Mary (2019) Women Rowing North: Navigating Life's Currents and Flourishing As We Age. Bloomsbury Press.

Northrup, Christiane (2016), *Goddesses Never Age: The Secret Prescription for Radiance, Vitality, and Well-Being*. Hay House.

Grierson, Bruce, (2014) *What Makes Olga Run?: The Mystery of the 90-Something Track Star and What She Can Teach Us About Living Longer, Happier Lives*. Henry Holt & Co.

Lawrence, Holly (2019), Can Wisdom Protect Against Loneliness? Next Avenue blog April 11.
https://www.nextavenue.org/can-wisdom-protect-against-loneliness/

Musgraves, Kacey -
https://youtu.be/GZfj2lr3GgQ

Chapter 16

Tharp, Twyla (2017) Keep It Moving: Lessons for the Rest of Your Life, Simon & Schuster.

Coughlin, Joseph F. (2019), "Old age" is made up—and this concept is hurting everyone." MIT Technology Review. August 21.

Applewhite, Ashton (2019) This Chair Rocks: A Manifesto Against Ageism. Celadon Books.

Bernhard, Toni. (n.d.) Young people are treated as if their health issues can't possibly be chronic. Love What Matters Blog. https://www.lovewhatmatters.com/the-extra-burdens-faced-by-young-people-with-chronic-illness/

Glicksman, Allen (2015), quoted in Farrell, Chris,   Aging Populations Are Good for the Old and the Young, Next Avenue Blog. June 25.

Retrieved from https://www.nextavenue.org/aging-populations-are-good-for-both-the-old-and-the-young/

Cathy Goodwin

Printed in Great Britain
by Amazon